D1564691

Surprised
By peace

Surprised
By peace

edited by Mary Britton

"I will have mercy, and I will have compassion
on whom I will have compassion."
Romans 9:15

PressOn Publications
FORT LAUDERDALE, FLORIDA

Surprised
By peace

Published by **PressOn Publications**
PO Box 550363, Ft. Lauderdale, FL 33355

First paperback printing, 2002
Library of Congress Control Number: 2002106999

Cover design © 2002 Britton
Cover photo, Blackwater Sound, Key Largo, Florida © 2002 Britton

Printed in the United States of America
ISBN 0-9721883-0-4

Table of Contents

Acknowledgments 9

Introduction 11

Angels in Texas? 15

Dear God 23

Thank God I'm a Country Girl 29

The "C" Word 37

Long Distance Runner 41

I Am What I Am 47

Desert Sunrise 51

You're in the Army Now 61

Prepare for Takeoff 67

God Makes Me Laugh 75

The Odd Christian Out 81

I Am the Mother of a Gay Son 91

Jesus Loves Cowboys 95

Choosing the High Road................................... 109

Liberty 113

Small Steps First 123

Who Can Be Against Me? 129

Hate Is Not a Family Value 137

America, America 141

What Is a Nice Jewish Doctor
Doing in a Book Like This? 149

"Differently-Abled".. 159

Freedom Behind Bars 171

It's Always Something 181

Does the End Justify the Means? 187

Light From the Pages of Tolstoy 191

You've Got Mail 205

Invitation 219

Order Form 221

Order Form 223

Acknowledgments

Thank you to the contributors who spent hours of time out of their busy lives to share their important stories. May the Lord richly bless you for your honesty and courage. Thank you to the ladies at Partner's who unwittingly inspired this project. To my dependable iMac friends, Carl, David, and John, thank you for your help and patience. Thank you Isabel for the Zip drive, which I've almost worn out. To all my friends that have encouraged me in the midst of computer glitches, equipment failures, and life's ups and downs, thank you for your support and prayers. Thank you BJ, Lucille, Nancy, Kathy, Mary Jane, Judy, and my cousins, Nikki, Cathy, Linda, and Carol for your longtime friendship, unconditional love and acceptance. Scott, thank you for your listening ear, words of wisdom and sense of humor. Thank you Jeannette for relentlessly reminding me to finish this book. And to my wonderful son, Max, thank you for always loving me, and being so proud of my every endeavor and accomplishment. A special thanks to my beloved partner, Jo, for your constant love, encouragement, editorial comments and suggestions. I couldn't have tackled this undertaking without you. You are a special inspiration to me and many others. Most importantly, I thank the Lord Jesus Christ for guiding my steps and keeping me close to His heart.

Introduction
by Mary Britton

There is a segment of society world-wide, namely homosexuals, that many well meaning people instantly, without much thought, categorize as perverted or evil. Many in organized church denominations swiftly dismiss them as *outcasts among outcasts.* They are said to have defiantly made *a choice,* going beyond the boundaries of God's acceptable norm, and are consequently consigned into one massive group condemned to hell.

Any effort made by homosexuals to defend themselves as valid and loving people are dismissed by many. Some have paid a great price to be free to be themselves, the way they believe they were created. They have been rejected by family and friends. Some have been kicked out of the churches they were raised in. They are blacklisted forever, unless they "repent" and quit being gay. If they get angry or frustrated they are criticized.

In living their everyday lives, gay people must choose the degree to which they are open and honest about their sexual identity. This is something the heterosexual never has to think about. Some gay people are courageously open. Others try their best to hide their "secret" from the entire world. The rest are constantly determining, throughout each and every day, whether they should or should not be open and honest, which is an exhausting and stressful way to live. It is well known in the realm of psychology that battered, ridiculed children act out in rebellion. Battered gay people sometimes act similarly and may become militant out of anger and frustration. When this happens, they are criticized even more and a vicious cycle ensues. Meanwhile, they are not like everyone else; they are inherently and truly different, and therein lies the dilemma.

In the following pages you will read short stories by everyday people who are not professional writers. They were invited to write their stories in hope that what they had experienced and learned would be of value to someone else, maybe you. They considered their efforts an opportunity to share their thoughts and faith. Some of the writers endured tremendous emotional stress reliving their past, and it was with great effort and the Spirit of God that they were able to complete the task.

The writers of these stories are the ones spoken of as unrepentant sinners, considered vile and base. Their accounts are full of astonishing trials, conflicts, and difficult journeys. They have grappled with society, the organized theology of the day, and the personal struggle of identity. At the same time, whole and honest people. The searching heart, the willing spirit, honesty, the desire for truth and forgiveness, and eventually, the dawning of a new found faith in the One True God are revealed in these pages. These accounts provide a momentary glimpse into the struggle of the homosexual in modern society trying to find peace of mind, peace with God, and peace with his fellow man.

Although these stories are about people with various backgrounds and experiences, there is a common theme throughout the pages of this book: God is real. As you read, you will be challenged spiritually and possibly surprised by the evidence of God's Spirit engaged in the intricate details of these lives. In the most unexpected ways, with the most unlikely people, God surprises us all with His peace, as He lives up to His grace and His character, confounding the (so-called) wise of this world by claiming the base things of the world, the despised, as His own.

Angels in Texas?

I thought the funeral would never end. As I looked at my mom in that casket, I just wanted to go home. Little did I know that this day was about to change the course of my life.

I was born the youngest of four children. My mother lived with the threat of heart failure all of her life and at the age of 40, her heart beat for the last time. I was 12 years old. My 15 year old brother and I were very close. My mom had encouraged us to always be there for one another and I clung to him as never before. Changes were happening so quickly that I could hardly keep up with them.

My father had always been a drinker, but now he was lost in the bottle and bars. I watched as the once loving man, my dad, turned into an abusive monster. My brother could not handle the beatings, so when the opportunity came to go live with my mom's sister, he gladly went. I could hardly blame him.

I felt that I had lost my mom, my dad (to alcohol), and now my brother. I became very bitter, began sniffing glue, drinking, and got into a lot of trouble. My mother's brother took me to live with him in Alabama, but that was short lived. About four months later, I was back home and things became more abusive than ever before.

Some years later, my aunt decided that my brother had adjusted well to living with them and perhaps I would too. So, off to South Carolina I went. My aunt and uncle were wonderful Christian folks, but very strict. I, on the other hand, was very rebellious. As one would imagine, it was quite an adjustment period for all of us. My uncle taught at the local Christian school in which I was enrolled shortly after my move to their home. The school was very regimented and I was not. They taught and spoke of God and talked about Jesus as our personal savior. "Savior from what?" I thought. He had not saved me from anything.

Church was more of the same. I heard about a love that I could not understand and wanted no part of. But one Sunday everything seemed different; I don't know how to explain it. Instead of only hearing words about God's love, I began to feel His love and embrace. Suddenly, I knew I wanted more of Him. So, when the preacher said that if anyone wanted to ask Jesus into their life he would pray with them, I didn't hesitate. My tired, angry and bitter heart was transformed that day. I was filled with love, hope and rest.

The school was still regimented, my uncle and aunt still very strict, and at church they still talked about a loving savior. My situation was still the same but the way I began to embrace life had changed dramatically. I studied very hard at the Bible school. I just could not learn enough about Jesus. At home, I helped with chores and had no desire to get into trouble.

Two years later things changed again. I was sent back home to my father's care, the old neighborhood, and public schools. But I went back with Jesus in my life. While the situation with my dad was the same (maybe worse), I was not afraid to live, to function, or to love.

Upon my return home, I found a great church and became a junior minister to the youth group. At school, I became involved with Youth for Christ and began speaking at meetings around our city. At home, I tried to share Jesus every chance I could.

I graduated from high school and took a job that required travel. After two years, I returned home from this job and became involved with street ministries.

This was my life until I was 23. Then I found myself in a relationship with a woman. I felt I needed to be honest with the ministries I was associated with. After much prayer, I decided I would share that I was a lesbian. The result was devastating. Christian people, whose lives I had become a part of, wanted nothing more to do with me. I was not welcomed at church, Bible studies, or prayer meetings. I was rejected and condemned. What was worse was that I bought into the condemnation. I knew that I couldn't change the fact that I was a lesbian. I believed them when they said Jesus didn't want me unless I changed. I turned from them and from God.

The next 17 years of my life were lived as though the sentence to death had already been pronounced. I became a walking dead person. I became addicted to drugs, every narcotic I could get, and became totally engulfed in the drug scene. But everyday I thought about Jesus. I had been so sure of His love, but all of those Christians could not be wrong, could they?

The last six years before I got clean, I became addicted to crack cocaine. I lost everything I had and knew if something didn't happen, I would lose my life. I became acutely aware of good and evil, and evil permeated my life. I did not want to die like this. So, at about 90 pounds, I desperately locked myself in my basement, determined to get clean or die.

I am not sure what actually took place in that basement. I do remember calling out to God in my pain and sickness. My first real awareness was being wrapped in a blanket, stained with my own body waste. I was not sure how long I had been there, or even where I was. But I was alive. I had lived through the worst of the withdrawals and had a lot of work ahead. Hidden in the recesses of my frail and bruised face, I saw eyes filled with life, struggling to survive. My thoughts drifted to Jesus. It was as though I could feel His love and acceptance; but all of those Christians that condemned me could not have been wrong, could they?

I went to a mental health center in my area that had a special program for addictions. I received support and counseling there for a few years. I found myself often talking to God, seeking His will regarding my sexuality. His answers for me came and they were clear.

Friends invited me to a Christian retreat in Texas, expenses paid. They were Christians who were gay, and the retreat was primarily for Christian gay folks. Well, I had never heard of such a thing. Gay people couldn't be born again believers, could they? So, off I went to Texas.

Upon my arrival, I met a little woman who was greeting people at the lodge where I was staying. She gave me a hug, stepped back, looked into my eyes, and said, "Oh, I already know you!" I thought, "Oh great, what have I gotten myself into? They are all wacky!" I put my luggage away and tried to make myself scarce. As I was sitting alone in a pavilion, guess who was heading my way but the little wacky woman. She came over, put her chair right in front of me, sat down and said, "Hope I did not alarm you when I said I already knew you. Please let me explain. When I was praying about this gathering, God gave me a message for you and He told me that I would know you when I saw you." At this point I knew for sure she was wacky, at least until I heard more of what she had to say. She continued, "Jesus has never stopped loving you and He wants you to know..." Then she spoke of a couple of things that happened in my life that I had never spoken aloud to anyone, ever.

She said that God wanted me to know that He understood, and forgave me, and still had a call on my life. He created me with divine purpose, just as I was. Whew, talk about blown away: that God would give a message for me to someone several states away and then send us both to Texas; this was all too wild! Well, God sure had my attention. The Holy Spirit spoke to me; "They stamped you invalid (not valid) and you became invalid (disabled). That was never my desire for you."

From that day forth, I have not been the same. My heart is to serve Jesus. I now pastor a church and most of the members are homosexual and born again believers. God has brought a wonderful spouse into my life who is also in the ministry. Together we share the love of Jesus with others.

Could all of those Christians that condemned me be wrong? Does Jesus really love me? His answer time and time again is yes!

Dear God,

Hey there! I hope this letter finds you well. I am sure you are wondering why I am writing you a letter, especially since I have never written to you before. Well, I was recently given the assignment of writing to you. In this assignment, I was posed the question: "When was the first time I sensed your presence in my life and describe some of the ways you have revealed yourself to me." Lord, this was a really difficult question and required a great deal of thought. My first reaction to this question was that I had never felt your presence, until recently, that is. For the past 19 years, I was far from the "model" Christian. Then I really began to reflect on this question and my life.

Ever since I can remember, I knew of your existence. As a child, I remember hearing many biblical stories about you. I went to church every Sunday, religiously (no pun intended). I even attended the most boring Sunday classes ever held on the face of your earth. But in all that time, I do not recall ever sensing your presence. Back then, going to church and Sunday school were part of life's routine, a routine I followed because of family and tradition. When I was around 16, my mother forced me to go on a weekend retreat sponsored by the Catholic Youth Group. Now, the key word here is *forced.* If you recall, I wanted no part of it and I was scared to death that it was going to be three straight days of "Sunday School Hell." To a 16 year old, that was a fate worse than death! Begrudgingly, I was blackmailed into going, and to my surprise, I actually enjoyed it. Looking back on it now, I can admit that it was even fun (but don't tell my mother!). It was on that weekend retreat that I first realized that you were more than a weekly routine or tradition. I realized that you were *God* and that you were real. I definitely grew closer to you and I found a new respect for you on that weekend. But still, I didn't feel your presence.

Over the next few years my faith grew, but I also began to question many teachings of the Church. You know teenagers; they think they know everything. I realize now that I was not questioning your Word (the Bible), but the Church's interpretation of it. Needless to say, it was a very confusing time for me.

Then, when I was 19, two tragic events happened in my life. In a split second, I lost two wonderful souls that meant more to me than life itself. In my youth, I could not understand how such a loving and merciful God could allow such tragic losses to occur. I was stunned. I became an emotional wasteland. In my grief, I blamed you for my loss. For this I am truly sorry. (You know, this is the first time that I have ever apologized to you for my behavior 20 years ago. I'm sorry it took me so long). I know that it was wrong to blame you, but my youth, my pain, and my lack of understanding of you, blinded me. The funny thing is that now I am so thankful to you for being with me at that time.

It wasn't until I sat down to write this letter that I realized this was the first time I felt your presence. On that tragic night, you were with me and filled me with strength. You also gave me a rare and beautiful gift. You let my best friend of 18 years die in my arms. She did not die alone and afraid. You gave me the opportunity to say I love you one last time. You let me tell her that she would always live inside my heart. You let me say good-bye. She did not die alone, scared, and in pain, but in my loving arms, with an indescribable peace. I will always be grateful for that gift and your presence. I have never thanked you for that. It's a little late, but thank you! Since that sad night so many years ago, I now realize that you have been with me numerous times. You let me walk away from a car accident when all logic says I should have died. You let me recover from an illness that all said was fatal. You have guided me through depression, sadness, fear, loneliness and even the happy times. Only now have I come to recognize how many times I have felt your presence in my life. What a wonderful feeling it is.

I look forward to understanding more about you and growing in spirit. I will try to live my life the best I can and try to be the person you want me to be. I thank you for the wonderful people in my life, the teachers you have sent me, my church, and my family. I thank you for giving us your only Son. Most of all, thank you for your love and your constant presence in my life.

Love,
Your Humble Servant
Tim

Thank God
I'm a Country Girl

I'm just a plain ol', down-home, traditional southern country woman. I believe in inviting the preacher over for a big Sunday dinner. I believe in treating folks the way you want them to treat you. Most importantly, I believe in God. Not believing in God was never my problem. My problem was that I didn't believe that God could possibly believe in me.

I was raised in church: actually, a series of churches. Small, rural, backwoods Pentecostal churches where "Thou shalt nots" were more important than "God loves you." We usually became involved with these churches after my parents received food, checks, and clothing from them. My father, an active alcoholic in his younger years, did not have a good track record when it came to employment, responsibility or maturity. My mother, often unable to work due to physical, emotional and mental illness, was the resourceful one in the family.

She found churches that helped us financially and/or with food. We attended these churches until somebody got mad at somebody else and we left to scout for the next church with a food pantry.

It was at these churches, where the women piled their locks atop their heads in the fashionable "Holiness prayer hair" style, and the men wore mustard colored polyester suits, that I learned about God. In spite of the "love God and country" theology of these extreme, rigid people, I witnessed and experienced multiple abuses, both inside and outside the church. To this day though, I still love the fire and the spirit of a Pentecostal church service, and I just love the singing -- just love it.

As a little girl, I feared thunderstorms because I thought each lightening bolt was straight from God and aimed for me. I really believed that God was a vengeful, punitive, shriveled up old man in the sky, who, like everyone else in my life, had given up on me.

At the age of 12, I decided that I was the only person I could count on. I began a pattern of using drugs and running away that eventually led to a life of heroine addiction, prostitution, crime and total spiritual bankruptcy. I was in the midst of this absolute chaos, which I called my life, when I realized that I was a lesbian. Believing this was another way to defy society, with all its "shoulds and should nots," I embraced and exploited my sexuality, and added it to my list of reasons why nobody, including God, loved or accepted me.

Looking back, I know now that God always loved me. It was I who did not accept God. Because I did not love myself, I believed there must be something terribly wrong with anyone who loved or accepted me, including God. Sometimes I still struggle with that old, sick thinking, until I remind myself that no matter what, God does love me and so do the important people in my life. I have to love even those who don't love me or else I'll become as they are, bitter and self-focused, with no joy. I do not want to be like that. Jesus said, "I came that they may have life, and have it abundantly." I personally believe that joy is the abundance to which He was referring. Spiritually empty people cannot feel joy.

My first hint that God really did love me came at the age of 18. Addicted to opiates and involved in an abusive, dysfunctional marriage, I gave birth to my son, who weighed only two pounds and twelve ounces. When I looked at him in the incubator, so tiny, with no eyelashes, eyebrows, or fingernails, I felt like the scum of the earth. I had this precious gift from God, finally someone who might be able to love me and I had already abused him. I prayed fervently that God would let him live and let me die. But God, being such a loving God, let this tiny little soul live, a medical miracle 25 years ago. In spite of my illness, I loved my son and I took his survival as a sign that God loved me.

Part of the reason for my self-hatred was my intense dislike of my appearance, which I projected onto every person I ever met. I was always big and hated my size. At age 16, I had a stroke while using IV cocaine and crystal methamphetamine, which resulted in the right side of my face being drawn and uneven. I felt self-conscious and ugly. Every person in my life who said they loved me, except for my boy, called me fat, one-eyed, or ugly at one time or another. I really thought I was so grotesque that even God could not look upon me.

I was 24 when I met someone special. She was different from anyone I had ever known before. She was somewhat street wise and had endured much abuse in her life also. However, she believed in God and had a sweet and loving spirit. She thought I was beautiful. I was fascinated by her trust in God and I knew, deep down inside, that I wanted to be like that. She was the catalyst that helped me to reconnect with God; a kind, loving God who was a parent and not a tyrant.

God brought wonderful people into my life at the times I needed them most and still continues to do so. As a child in an unhealthy environment, God gave me a grandma, a proud Cherokee woman who was my tower of strength. She was not a church-going woman, but she was a worshiper. She believed in God, in herself, and in me. She taught me that God wants us to be joyful. She told me that God loved Indians too, a sentiment not shared by the general population and certainly not taught in my Pentecostal Sunday school.

Then there are the friends God gave me throughout the years, each of them sent with a special message for me, a lesson to learn and a blessing to receive. For them, I am also grateful.

I guess if I had to describe the core of my spiritual beliefs in one word, it would be gratitude. Today, I know that there is a God, in whose image I am made, who loves me and blessed me with a beautiful spirit. I know that I had lessons to learn so that I could grow, and I know that God was never punishing me. God was strengthening me and polishing me. For all of this I am grateful. I know that no matter what happens and no matter how often humans have deserted and abandoned me, I will never be alone.

I am grateful that I didn't die in a back alley with a tourniquet around my arm and a rusty old syringe in my hand. I did not contract HIV, even though I shot dope with people who later tested HIV positive. I am grateful I didn't spend my whole adult life in prison, like I probably should have. I am grateful that after I lost custody of my son due to addiction, God returned him to me. I am grateful that I now have a career that is not crime focused, and I'm grateful that my home is focused on Christ.

You could possibly convince me that the world will end tomorrow. You could possibly convince me that Christianity is not popular these days. But you will never convince me that any person is too low for God to pick up because I was that person. I am that person and God has been good to me, and good for me. For that I am grateful. My life is blessed today - mighty blessed.

The "C" Word

This is dedicated to all the women who have known the fear of cancer. To all others this is an issued warning to have your mammograms, despite what your doctors say about your age. My first mammogram was done at the early age of 29. It wasn't soon enough.

In February 1995, I received some disturbing news. My family and I heard one of the most frightful, dire statements a doctor can make: "Christina, you have breast cancer." Oh no, how could this be? Just two years prior to the exact day, I had my first mammogram and all was clean, they said. Now I hear this six-letter word ringing in my ears: cancer. Not just one type of cancer, but two different, very aggressive cancers.

I looked around the room at the worried faces present. I heard an outburst of agonizing cries from my precious mother, sister, brother, and partner. How can I stop this pain for them? How can I make all this bearable for those hurting? Never once did that word actually register with me. I asked, "What do I do to rid myself of this?" The doctor replied, "Remove your whole right breast, nipple and all." "Okay," I said, "let's do it." I knew somehow, with God's help, I would prevail.

I never even cried, until the day of surgery. I was lying there awaiting my turn, all alone, cold, and yet without fear. All of a sudden I heard a voice nearby. I turned to look, and as my eyes came back across the room, I caught a glimpse of my breast. I thought this is it! The breast will never be the same. It was then that I said my farewells. I broke down, crying from deep within my soul. I cried out to God to please help me. I was embarrassed by my crying in public. I then heard His majestic voice say, "I will never leave you nor forsake you." In that very moment, I literally felt God's hand cover my shivering body like a warm blanket. I cried again, but this time out of gratitude. From then on, I no longer just read words in the Bible; I heard and felt God as never before through His Word.

After 12 1/2 hours of grueling surgery, I awoke to a nightmare: my scars. Mind you, the cancer never bothered me, but oh, those scars I had to live with now. My surgeon had butchered me. Days led to months and my scars were no better. Reconstructive surgery was a must. I went to another surgeon to have this done. He didn't have a very pretty canvas to start with, but he did the best he could. The results were a more desirable picture, one that made disrobing less painful and the occasional glance in the mirror less agonizing.

Being naked meant having to bear my soul. All the pain from start to present would have to be revealed. The surgery, scars, cancer and the breakup with my partner were just too much. I experienced a lot of loneliness. What was I to do? Thank God for real friends. God always knows what He is doing. Trust me, I have survived it all.

I have failed at many things in my life, but God never has. By the grace of God I started dating again, despite how painful it was. My family and friends surrounded me with love and understanding, not pity.

Less than two weeks ago (as I write this), five years after my first experience with cancer, I have just had my left breast removed due to question-able cysts. I again have received God's gracious healing. This time all was benign. I've had many scars these past five years, but God still gently reminds me that He hasn't left me.

___ Christina

To all of my loving family and friends: I could never convey my utmost gratitude and undying love for all of you. Please accept my humbled thanks for your support and encouragement. May God bless you with His richest blessings continually. I love you all, more than you could ever know.

Long Distance Runner

As far back as I can remember, love was ever present in my family. It's easy to give love if you've been raised in it.

My mother was a preacher's kid. She taught us about a loving God and how to love life. At any given moment, our house would be filled with her rich voice that ranged from soprano to a low tenor. She tried to teach me to sing hymns. Unfortunately, as patient as she was, I never got the knack of carrying a tune. I recall churches we attended and Bible study groups. That was a major part of our lives. God was always the focus in my life for as long as I can remember.

My husband's story is a little different. Bob was born so tiny that he was considered for the *Guinness Book of World Records,* in 1967. Someone once told me that if you get a grandma to pray for you, the request is as good as granted. Bob's grandmother dedicated his life to God the day he was born. Oh, he didn't know it then, but God had heard her request. She held this tightly in her heart and watched as he grew.

Growing up was not easy for Bob, a kid with cerebral palsy and a family that wasn't sure what to do with him. He was nearly drowned at eight years old, in the family pool. His dog rescued him! He also endured other various mishaps, including being stuffed in a dryer, being rendered unconscious by a hammer blow, and coming in contact with an electrical fence. His father, an affluent businessman, occasionally disciplined harshly, until welts appeared from the beatings. When Bob was 11 years old, that chapter ended when his father died.

Bob's mother, incapacitated by grief, was unable to care for the family. Bob moved in with his sister Diane, to allow some time for healing. Diane loved the Lord and encouraged Bob to get involved in church. The whole family was involved on a daily basis with church activities. Bob sensed a calling to the ministry when he was 16. He knew what he had to do but kept saying, "Who me? I can't." Bob started running from the Lord.

We first dated when Bob was 18. His church did not like the difference in our ages, and felt that he should leave the church. He was confused with why God would call him and yet shut doors. Where was the love that this church had shown in the beginning? God simply said, "Not here."

Bob, disenchanted, told me God could not use him "the way he was." God must have made a "mistake," he rationalized. However, in the back of Bob's mind, he knew that God was calling him. Instead, Bob decided to instruct for the Red Cross, ignoring the call to ministry. A nurse told him he could never administer CPR because of his physical condition. However, Bob not only to learned CPR, but became an instructor for both CPR and AIDS prevention.

One night a young man dying of AIDS attended one of Bob's classes. This young man had been shunned because he was gay. His own family feared him because he had AIDS. Bob, touched by this man's plight, finally stopped running from God and prayed, "Lord what do you want me to do?"

God told Bob to tell them that He loves them and that they can find peace in His Son. Soon after, couples, singles and families ravished by AIDS began approaching Bob for help.

Hope Ministries was established to help meet their needs, and to reach out to hospitals. AIDS takes not only the individual, but also the family. The reactions of families to this illness were varied. Some families accepted, some denied, and some encouraged the sick to take their own lives for their "sin."

A turning point for Bob came through a family with AIDS that he was ministering to. Both parents and their adopted son had AIDS. The biological parents had tried "recreational" drugs at a party, and their son was born with AIDS. They sent the baby to the "queer" uncles to raise, almost as a punishment. A more loving family is hard to find; their last six months were hard for all of us to watch. The first parent died of a heart attack, while the son was being instructed in CPR over the phone. The little boy was 11 when he went home to be with God. The third found his life so unbearable and lonely, he took his life, while Bob was frantically trying to find out where he was located so he could send help. Out of state, alone, and terminally ill, a bullet to the head seemed to be the solution. Those final sounds of gun-shot still haunt Bob. Did God want Bob to have a deeper insight into the people that he ministered to?

One day Bob was attacked in a parking lot by an individual wielding a needle. For the next year, Bob underwent the HIV tests, took the medications, and we practiced all the precautions. After three tests, he was confirmed HIV negative. What a relief. We had new empathy for those suffering with AIDS and those anxiously awaiting test results.

Bob has a heart to share the gospel and would like to be "on the road" more often, but he is a lot quicker to stop these days and let God lead him rather than run ahead of Him. Sometimes the road is steep and there are many pressures, but Bob has learned to await the Lord's direction. Now Bob invites God to pick out his running shoes...and God even ties the laces!

__ Coleen Forte

Bob and Coleen Forte have been married for 17 years. They are the founders of Hope Ministry Family Fellowship, located on Hamilton Street, in Allentown,

Pennsylvania. The church is a member of the national Alliance of Christian Churches, and welcomes all people. Pastor Bob's congregation is a mix of homosexual and heterosexual believers. Their motto is based on John 3:16, which states: "...whosoever believes in the Lord Jesus Christ shall be saved." (KJV)

I Am What I Am

I am a young black woman, raised Catholic, and always felt I was damned to hell. As a young girl, I realized that I was *different*, and I prayed to God everyday to make me *right* (make me a boy). As I grew, I started to understand myself better and realized, through schooling and church, that I was a sinner. I eventually came to the conclusion that, if my only sin was being who I am, than I would gladly pay the price. Maybe God would have mercy on my soul and send me to purgatory.

By the time I reached my twenties, I had read about numerous religions. Each one had negative things to say about gay people. I never thought about reading the Bible.

I met a black, gay couple who spoke of becoming pastors of a new church. It was the first time I identified with someone else. These women loved the Lord. It moved something in me, and I started to pray like I did when I was a child. God started to work with me. I moved from one job to another, and in that process, He placed people in my life that were gay and also loved the Lord Jesus Christ.

One day, while reading the Bible, I noticed a verse that said, "Before I formed you in the womb I knew you." Can you imagine how I felt when I read that? Everyone had said He hated me for being gay. Not only did He love me, but He knew me before I was born, and I was His creation.

I wept and wept for hours. I had held back tears for years. For so long I had pretended that I didn't care about anything, and now, finally, as I sat there crying, I was not trying to control my emotions and all the pain from the past. The tears streamed down my face. With this new knowledge, I started to attend different churches, hoping to find a home where I could hear God's truth. God guided me back to that original couple I had met previously. They were now pastoring a growing church. I began to participate in the services and found friends that I felt at home with.

I thank God for having His hand on me, even when I turned my back on Him, and for loving me, when I wasn't able to love myself. Now, no matter what, I know I have a personal relationship with Jesus Christ. I have found peace with the God of the universe.

___Mesha

Mesha continues to worship at the same church for the past two years. She is actively involved in the church and teaches the Bible to children.

Desert Sunrise

My name is Axel. I was born in Puerto Rico, in 1963. My family was a typical middle class family, with the common troubles of today's American family. Our household was tormented by the consequences of alcoholism and co-dependency. We struggled, as neither of my parents sought out professional help or spiritual guidance. However, all three children were brought up in an otherwise loving and resourceful environment.

At a very early age I knew I was somehow different from the rest of my playmates. Growing up, I wondered why I was different. But the answers were far from being found. To my family and friends, I was a perfect kid, because I learned to please my parents and society and meet the requirements to be acceptable to all.

For fear of rejection, I held back feelings of wanting to be an openly gay person. At about age 12 or 13, I asked my dad, "What if you had a gay son?" He replied, "I would kill him!" Mother, on the other hand, sensed my affinity to her and suddenly closed herself off to me, with cold, evasive treatment, wanting to make me "a man."

I grew up feeling isolated, so I searched for a Higher Power. I tried many religious denominations but something was missing. The more I went to church, the more I felt condemned. Fear of God took me over and I thought: if we sin just by thinking and not even executing an act, then I am a hopeless sinner. But I persevered and found people I could study the Bible with. The Bible studies were conducted under a specific denomination. Bible verses were often taken out of context and not studied in their true historic settings. However, I was not aware of this at that time and wondered why I was having so much difficulty with their teachings. I was far from discovering the greater truths of the Scriptures. I finally decided to try to be the best I could and went on with my life, leaving behind my Bible studies and the search for a religion that could provide me with spiritual comfort.

For years I lived life as most people do, conforming to a set of morals and implementing learned behavior. I grew distant from God and lived life the "easy way." I moved away from home and friends, far from the land where I was born. My set of values crumbled as I met different people and found ways to escape reality. After I finished college and tasted financial independence, I felt it was my time to be free. Drugs and alcohol became essential during my leisure time, and I played hard.

Bad habits and addictions followed me to professional school. I did strive to become a better person, someone my parents could be proud of. But alcoholism finally took its toll on me during my first year of dental school. Depression set in and I became trapped in a vicious circle of drinking binges, hitting rock bottom. The stress that came with professional school was unbearable, and marijuana and alcohol provided me with immediate sedation. It was like taking a high interest loan: enjoy it now, but suffer later.

Anxiety, and again, a feeling of inadequacy, marked the days I spent in professional school. Toward the end of the day all I could think about was how long before I could go drink that beer. But after I drank, the relief wasn't really fulfilling. I looked at the people around me and it seemed they had nowhere else to go either. The conversations had no depth, and the hours just passed. I stayed in bars for extended hours into the night, for fear of going home to myself.

As I became a regular at local bars, it became easy to adopt patterns of behavior that were once foreign to me. Such behaviors included a constant search for someone to have sex with and acquiring recreational drugs that would make me desirable to be with. It was a slow process of desensitization. Things that I once considered wrong became acceptable. I had built a sand castle supported by a straight pin and it was all soon going to crumble.

I did have a few sort of stable relationships, but they all dissolved. There was always someone richer or better looking than I was. My popularity grew as I gave into the whole gay scene. With a newly acquired body that took hours to build, the hunt for the next trick was at the reach of my palms. One year of dental school was sacrificed. My self-esteem was shot to pieces. I was once again trapped.

With stern determination, I made some hard decisions. I left behind my old friends, my old habits, the bars, and my search for a companion. However, I continued to smoke marijuana in "moderation."

Just like it happened yesterday, I remember one winter my sister came to visit. She was the only family member who knew about my sexuality and was somewhat supportive. As I picked her up at the airport I blew some smoke out. She looked at me with concern and asked, "When are you quitting that stuff?" Very irritated, I replied, "Never." That incident played and replayed in my mind for days after she was gone. She had always been so supportive and her question was filled with care and genuine concern. It all triggered a memory of who I was and where I came from. It sort of put me back in touch with myself.

Dental school days came to a conclusion and life went on. The happiness of becoming a doctor was very short lived. I obtained my license, moved to the state of my choice, and began working, but nothing gave me a sense of satisfaction. Sadness just followed me. A few months after my big move to Florida, a good friend died. Unable to travel at the time, I was disturbed that I could not be there for his family and friends. At that time, someone approached me and extended an invitation to go to a small local church. He had suggested that I enter a prayer request for the comfort of family and friends. Finding it a good idea, I submitted the prayer request.

It was there, in that little storefront church, with no luxuries or fancy decorations, that I found the enormous peace that I lacked for decades. The prayer request wasn't read aloud, but hymns were sung by untrained voices with willing hearts. I remember it so clearly, the voices singing "alleluia." Something took me over and I was suddenly flooded with happiness in my heart. I knew then and there I had just found a place where the Holy Spirit was present. As I cried, many came to comfort me, thinking I was sad for the loss of my friend. Instead, I was so happy to just be there and participate in the joy and healing power of the Holy Spirit.

This is not a testimony of someone who has found God and is now a Christian. It is the testimony of someone who always believed in Christ, but lost faith and was lost in the world. Does that mean that I am now immune to the temptations of the world? Certainly not! What I can testify is that I have found a source of study, a place where I learn the truth, unblemished by traditionalism. A place where I learned about God's will and the liberation, rather than the condemnation, that He has extended to humankind, through His Son Jesus. These truths are there for all of us to discover. No matter what we think of ourselves or others, we are all capable of finding peace with our Creator. He does not take away joy and happiness, but actually gives us more.

As I grew stronger in faith, it became clear to me that life without Christ, while possible, is as empty and desolate as a desert without a horizon.

A long time ago I learned that we should love our neighbors as ourselves. What if we don't love ourselves? How could we love someone else when we don't even like who we are?

Christ, who died for our sins and resurrected, has saved us all with unconditional love. He presents us clean and perfect to our Father, who is in heaven (so much for my feelings of inadequacy). I now stand in awe of the change that has taken place in my life and the strength that continues to grow in my heart. I now stand in awe as the Lord continues to work in the lives of people around me, as well as in mine. To simply hear these truths is one thing. What is essential for change is to understand what these truths actually mean, internalize them, and incorporate them into our lives.

I now look back and feel as if I lived my life blindfolded and without direction. To anyone out there reading this testimony, your life is part of a greater whole. You are loved and cared for. Chances are that your experience is not as unique as you may think, for we are all human and vulnerable to similar things. There is hope, however, for all of us, no matter how we feel about ourselves. Experience the joy shared by those who have discovered the Grace of God.

___Axel Martinez, D.M.D.

Axel has a growing dental practice in South Florida. He continues to grow spiritually and encourages others to place their faith in Christ Jesus. He does not preach to others, but instead, shares his story and the faith, hope and joy he has found in Christ.

You're in the Army Now

I was raised as a Reform Jew, verging on "whatever." We went to synagogue on holidays, just long enough to show our faces, mostly on the street outside, where we could socialize. My mother was brought up orthodox, but was not educated in Judaism, so it didn't really mean much to her outside of the social aspect. I had gone to some classes, but was put off by the rabbis. One rabbi pinched my cheek one time too many, and the others wouldn't bother answering my questions because I was female.

I searched for spiritual direction. For a time in my life I was an atheist. At another time, I was deeply involved in a mind control group that was a front for the occult.

While I was involved with this group, in 1973, I met a woman named Dusty Pruitt. She was my Army recruiter. As I got to know her as a friend, and after we recognized each other as gay, she began talking to me about Jesus. I was pretty antagonistic: in all, we spent two and a half years arguing about religion. At one point she lent me a book by Hal Lindsey. I had just begun to read it when I went to one of the mind control group's higher level meetings. I'm a fairly logical and grounded person, but that night I saw something that changed a whole lot of things for me. I mentioned the book to a fellow at the meeting. In his eyes, for just a heartbeat, I saw something that I can only describe as pure evil. It was as if I had been given a glimpse behind the curtain of the occult. It frightened me so much that I fled the room and never went back.

Dusty invited me to her church soon after that incident and I accepted. It seemed that my mind had been opened to more than just the reality of evil. It was really the strangest thing. The Spirit of God was present in that church, in that service. I had never encountered *that* Spirit before. I continued to attend the church periodically, when I was home on leave. In December 1975, I made the decision to accept Jesus as my Messiah.

At that point in her life, Dusty told me that she had been going through a crisis of faith that year. She prayed that God would send her a sign that what she was preaching to gay folks, (that they could be gay and Christian), was okay, and that she wasn't misdirecting people to hell. I was that sign.

It took me another eight years to realize that I still wasn't at peace. Nothing in my life had really changed, especially my continued fascination with the occult, which kept me from reading the Scriptures. Then friends sent me to a straight, fundamentalist preacher who didn't know that we were gay. The minister and I talked and prayed for two hours that afternoon. I confessed every sin I could think of (without mentioning the "h" word, since I didn't consider it a sin). What happened then is almost the stuff of clichés, except that it really happened. I sensed a presence, as real to me as the room I was in. The presence washed me clean inside in a way I'd never experienced before or since, and planted in me an incredible joy that has never left.

I promised the Lord that I would get rid of my vast library of books about the occult. It took me only an hour the next morning to destroy 1,500 books. During the next seven years I read the Scriptures continually, which I had never been able to do before because of the occult books.

Over the years since that experience, I have had periods of doubt because of the constant badgering from the anti-gay religious forces. I've studied Scripture and prayed over the issue, and God dealt with me each time. The last time I had doubts, I packed an overnight case and booked a room at a local Catholic retreat center. I planned to stay until God answered my question about homosexuality. I arrived, prayed over a couple of other issues, then settled in. Silly me. I received God's answer immediately. He told me there was no problem and to go home. So I did.

Much of the pain comes from those with whom I most agree theologically and with whom I would most love to work: people in the Messianic Jewish movement. It hurts that these people are so rejecting of me as a gay person. One time I prayed that God would show me a way to work with them, but He told me no, that there were Jews among the gay people. Funny thing, the next Sunday there were three Jewish people who came to our MCC service for the first time. One still remains a friend.

I currently belong to a community church, basically evangelical, reaching out to glbt people in the world. My partner, who had been an MCC minister for many years, and I have just celebrated our 17th anniversary. My family is close and loving. I still pray that they will come to know Jesus as I have come to know Him, welcoming and kind.

_____Arlene Robbins

Prepare for Takeoff

"How do you reconcile the fact that you are a homosexual, yet claim to be a Christian?" I was recently asked this question. Many religious and right wing groups have judged homosexuals to damnation and the majority of their followers either agree or have been biased to believe that as fact. Of course, I was taught those same values. Not so much from my parents, but from our culture, on the playground, in school, etc. But now, after carefully searching the Scriptures and praying endlessly about the fact that I am a lesbian, I have no doubts that not only does God love me as I am, but indeed, He created me the way I am for His purpose.

I realized I was gay 14 years before I accepted Jesus Christ as my Lord and Savior. At that young age, I had never heard of sex, gay or straight, or anything else related to these subjects. But I was keenly aware that I was different than anyone I had ever known or seen. I was young but still realized that people, including my own family, were probably going to have some difficulty accepting me if I "confessed." So I had my first secret from the rest of the world. It wasn't too hard to keep. Being a tomboy, my best friends growing up were guys, and, of course, later they were boyfriends. Looking back, I think the rest of the world must have been in denial about my sexuality.

My parents married in the Catholic Church (my father's background) and agreed to raise their children in Catholicism. They insisted we attend catechism and mass until we were confirmed. I had a lot of questions. The nuns struggled to convince me why I had to confess to a mortal man, why I couldn't eat fish on Friday, why I couldn't interlace my fingers while praying ("God won't hear you like that"), and why I had to keep other Catholic rules.

I always felt I knew God personally, if not intimately. But I didn't read the Bible. The

Catholic Church at that time almost discouraged its use. Instead, we were told what to believe. I fought it; it never seemed right to me. Surely, if God was love, He would be more about joy and laughter than fire and brimstone and a long list of don'ts.

I wasn't raised in a Christian home. A "good" home, yes, but I didn't learn about Jesus Christ, the Bible, or prayer; we were just religious. The only thing I remember learning through Catholicism and my folks' fulfilled vows was the importance of keeping one's promise. After the age of seven, I no longer attended mass or church again, other than maybe Easter or Christmas services. Therefore, I never received the damning message about homosexuality but I knew I would be rejected by my peers and be an outcast of sorts if I ever revealed who I was deep within. That was enough for me to remain quiet. But I never believed that God had rejected me.

Being raised in an Air Force family, we moved often. By high school, I found myself living in the Bible belt of South Carolina, with raging hormones. In all my experiences to that point, I had never (knowingly) met another gay person. Not surprising, being a military brat, I was pretty rowdy at that stage of my life. During my junior year, I was attracted to a new set of friends. I loved their parents and enjoyed hanging around their homes. What I didn't know was they were Christians. I still partied with my old friends and took some grief for hanging around conservative "goody-two shoes." I didn't care. It was relaxing, fun, and something else I just couldn't put my finger on.

Late in my senior year of high school (March 26, 1977), my friend's mom talked to me about Jesus Christ. She had done this before and also read Scripture to me. This particular day was like any other, except deep in my soul, I felt and *knew* I was hearing something very sacred and special. After I asked God to forgive my sins, and asked Jesus into my heart, I had the most overwhelming feeling and began shaking and laughing. I knew my life had just changed forever and I had such a peace within. I told everyone: first my parents, then sisters, then old friends; whoever would listen!

I knew I was going to be watched and judged once I professed my new found faith. I was pretty popular with the partying group, which ridiculed me and doubted what had transpired. In a loving way, I just said "watch." I too was eager to see what God would do in my life. I quit drinking, smoking, and cussing. My demeanor also changed and I became a better listener and more patient. At the time, this was quite a remarkable change in my behavior. Only God could have enabled me with the power to change so greatly. There was no effort or struggle on my part. Joy and happiness were my total experience.

How do I know that Jesus really came into my heart? The peace. Had you known me as a kid, you would have thought I had a charmed life. I loved my parents and school. I was popular, captain of all the sports teams I played on, etc. But *nothing* can compare with having a personal relationship with the Lord Jesus, knowing I am His child and that He loves me unconditionally. I speak with Him at all times. Better yet, He speaks with me when I need Him the most.

I admit, as a Christian, I have not always been so intimately connected to God. It has been cyclical, always at my doing. Through countless hours of prayer and Bible study I've learned to apply the principles of trust and obedience. When I ask God for guidance, my life glides by gently. Do I still have problems? Of course, I do. But now I accept God's assistance.

So, back to the original question: "How do you reconcile the fact that you are a homosexual, yet claim to be a Christian?" It's not my intent to reiterate all the literature I've read by theologians in support of the fact that being gay and Christian is not only possible, but created by God. Instead, I'd like to share some of God's truths and promises. The Apostle Paul tells us, "There is therefore now no condemnation for those who are in Christ Jesus." He also was "...convinced that neither death, nor life, nor angels, nor rulers, nor things present, nor things to come, nor powers, nor height, nor depth, nor anything else in all creation, will be able to separate us from the love of God in Christ Jesus our Lord." What wonderful truths to cling to!

I have debated with condemning, straight Christians who are more articulate, educated, and persuasive than I. But no matter who "wins" the debate, the Bible tells me God loves me no matter what. As long as I believe Him to be my Lord and put my salvation in His blood, I am counted among His children and nothing can separate us!

Unlike people who abandon us when we tell them who we really are (I lost some friends when I came out), God never leaves or abandons us. My courage to come out came from the Lord, who said, "The truth shall set you free." I find comfort in the fact that the world despised Jesus too. My relationship with Him soothes my soul and gives me joy everyday. I encourage you to go directly to the source, God Himself, and begin your search.

___ Kathi Durst

Kathi graduated from the Air Force Academy in 1981. She served as a T-38 flight instructor and was the only female captain in this position at the time. She was on active duty with the Air Force for seven years. For the past 14 years, Kathi has been a pilot for American Airlines, flying 737 jets internationally.

Kathi is one of the founding members of the Church of The Holy SpiritSong in Deerfield Beach, Florida. She serves as an active member and elder. Kathi and her partner, also a believer in Christ, have been in a loving, committed relationship for six years.

God Makes Me Laugh

I used to pray for God to allow me to leave this world. There was only one thing I thought about: the world was sick. Back then I didn't know that it was me, not the world, that was sick. I couldn't seem to face life and just wanted to die.

Life as an adolescent was like being in a fantasy world. When I should have been learning to interact with others, I ended up, at a young age, living with someone who introduced me to the world of drugs and kept me isolated.

I ran away from home at 16 and was considered a troubled child by my family. I was simply a kid that had never received childhood direction. The only option I felt I had was to run away and start my own life. I jumped on a bus headed for New York and basically lived on the streets of Manhattan for six months. When I couldn't tolerate it any longer, I made my way to Florida. I met an older guy who influenced me in a very negative way, but it took me seven years to figure that out. I finally got out of that bad relationship and got my own apartment. Something was missing in my life. I just thought it was a relationship. I spent many hours in bars searching for that person. I received a lot of DUI's back then. I was an avid wind surfer, and a bad day at the beach was better than a good day at work. I still cannot figure out how I graduated from electrical apprenticeship school.

I was diagnosed with HIV in 1986. I began to attend a church, but when I realized they did not preach the Bible I left. Everyone back then was giving up on God. Remember the bumper stickers that said, "God is dead"? Yuppies, crystals, the women's movement, and 1-900-GIRLS were in. I did not blend into the world as I saw it. It seemed to me that the world was in serious trouble. And I was living my life aimlessly. In 1994, things went downhill with my health. I developed serious symptoms and ailments, which further compromised my immune system and the HIV. I was having a more difficult time getting to work, but I never realized that I needed to be at home. I went on a two year binge of drugs and alcohol to hide from reality and wound up in rehab. No longer able to work full time, I lost my home, but I hung in there. But everything was a mess and getting worse by the minute.

I met someone in a restaurant that said they had a friend that needed some electrical work. I did some work for this man and found out that he was a preacher. He invited me to his church. I was uncomfortable in the church, but the people accepted me for just me and they wanted to see me again. I learned that people were not uncaring.

I asked Jesus to come into my life and began to get clean. I attended a Bible study every week just to break with being home alone. I would pray constantly in order to stay focused. I learned about Jesus. I think it's cool to have an invisible friend at 36 years old. Things I prayed about were answered. It was strange that every time I got stuck God would make me laugh. One time I was driving around, sort of doubting the things that I had learned about Christ, when I saw just what I needed on a billboard that read "What I need is GOD." Answers to questions or doubts would just pop up in strange places. I couldn't do anything else but laugh. I never smiled before, so I assumed that it was Jesus who was making me smile. Sometimes I would even crack up laughing. Something came over me, like nothing I ever knew before; I was not alone anymore. When I fall He catches me. I don't curse, smoke, or get upset at trivial things anymore. I do not drink or do drugs. That kind of amazes me.

Today, I pray for others to find what I found in Christ.

Jack passed away from cirrhosis of the liver with HIV complications on December 14, 2001. He wrote his prayers down every day and even talked to strangers about how Christ had changed his life. Jack had a dry sense of humor. He was able to laugh and joke even facing death. Jack had a difficult journey as he courageously fought to live, and he found great comfort and peace in Jesus Christ up until the moment of his death. He inspired many who knew him. After his passing his journal was discovered. It was filled with daily, handwritten prayers of thanks and genuine loving thoughts regarding God, Jesus, his family and friends.

The Odd Christian Out

At times I have found myself vacillating between two closets. Closet number one obscures my sexual orientation from an otherwise inviting and nourishing Christian church. Closet number two conceals my zealous and passionate Christian identity from a gay and lesbian community that views Christianity as fostering oppression, discrimination, hatred, and even murder of homosexuals.

It is not uncommon for a gay or lesbian person to ask me, "Don't you feel like a hypocrite endorsing a religion that denies your basic existence?" A hypocrite, no. But terribly lonely, yes. A loneliness so overwhelming that, when coupled with the power of Christian peer pressure, became a catalyst for life-altering decisions that had the potential for everything from self-destruction to personal fulfillment.

In the 1980's, I set out to resolve this dilemma by arduously searching for other Christ-centered, Bible-reading, gay and lesbian people. My efforts yielded sadly limited results. Starving for fellowship with other disciples, I shifted gears, gravitating toward the abundant invitations from the evangelical community with its overflow of passionate young people longing to live for Christ.

Though accepted into an evangelical church, I continued to anguish over the conflict between my lesbian identity and a faith tradition that abrasively denounced my "lifestyle." My pastor and a few close friends knew I was a lesbian; I'm still not sure how many others also knew. I didn't hide my sexual identity, but I didn't broadcast it either.

More than anything, I was searching for a solution that would terminate this spiritual battle. I became more desperate when my parents, traditional Catholics, discovered I was a lesbian and disowned me.

The solution I chose was to overcome my homosexuality by means of Christian support networks, biblical obedience, and eventually, heterosexual marriage. I vowed to surrender all to God with my sexual orientation topping the list. After all, most of my young adult life had involved making decisions without any serious biblical direction or prayerful discernment. Maybe one of those unenlightened decisions involved my homosexuality.

When I revealed this spiritual strategy to some of my longtime gay and lesbian friends, they responded with anger and rejection, accusing me of deserting them. I dismissed their anger, believing with all my heart, soul, and strength that God would change me. I kept ever before me these words of Scripture: "So if anyone is in Christ, there is a new creation: everything old has passed away; everything has become new."

My first step toward healing was to undertake a life of celibacy. But after a few years of avoiding intimate relations at all costs, I was so deeply depressed that I needed psychiatric medications. At that point I eliminated celibacy as an option.

My next attempt at healing began when my family and friends enthusiastically encouraged me to date men. So off I trekked to the Christian singles scene, where I met a kind and gentle Christian man who desired to date and eventually marry me, notwithstanding the full knowledge of my homosexual history. At last, a light in the lonely darkness.

I had convinced myself that heterosexual marriage represented the ultimate victory. I dreamed about proudly proclaiming myself as wife, mother, and former lesbian. This utopia was set in motion by a traditional church wedding, a white lace gown, an extended family, and of course, a portrait of Mom and Dad beaming with pride. Everyone was bubbling over with hope and happiness. Everyone except me. Six months after my storybook wedding something went awry. I watched an avalanche develop. Initially, tiny trickles of snow roll down the mountain as the pressure starts to build. Eventually a wall of white crushes everything in its path. This was the condition of my soul. First came a trickle of dishonesty, conflict, and guilt.

Intimacy with my new husband, both emotional and sexual, became increasingly difficult. I cried out to the Lord, "Oh my God, I'm failing! Please help me!" My husband and I sought Christian counseling and spent endless evenings pleading with God to make our marriage work, all to no avail. My inner pressure continued mounting until a full blown avalanche roared out the words, "You cannot live a lie!"

Was this the voice of God or my own deplorable character? Could I trust the message? An answer came when someone suggested saving the marriage by having children. The prospect of raising a child amid such chaos was unbearable for both of us. Three years after our wedding, my husband and I tearfully divorced. I believed I had failed.

Alone again, on a dark winter night in 1992, I heard in my heart a gentle, soft whisper: "My child, are you ready to receive the gift of who I created you to be?" I shuddered at the prospect that this could be the voice of God. *Wait a minute God! You mean my homosexuality is a gift? You mean you created me this way?*

My mind suddenly recalled a Bible passage: "Will what is molded say to the one who molds it: Why have you made me like this?" I began to wonder if I was unknowingly tampering with God's piece of clay. Was it possible to receive a message that was in direct opposition to the church leaders I trusted? After all, they said that they were proclaiming God's thoughts, not their own. But their message, "change who you are," was being nudged aside in my heart by another message, one that began to set me free.

The months following my divorce were a quiet time of emotional recovery. Solitude and prayerful reflection soothed my battered heart and soul. At last, the moment arrived when I finally admitted to myself that the truth of my identity as a lesbian had not changed because I had altered my circumstances.

A new dilemma arose. How could I lead a fruitful and God-centered life as a Christian lesbian? Would I have to sever relationships with most of my heterosexual Christian friends? Would my former gay and lesbian friends even

talk to me again? Would I ever find other gay
and lesbian Christians?

The next few months were inundated by
God's amazing grace. Doors opened to the discovery of gay and lesbian Christian organizations, a few affirming mainstream churches, and
a wonderful organization called PFLAG
(Parents/Friends of Lesbians and Gays). Gone is
the inner turmoil of dishonesty, shame, and
guilt. Instead, the Holy Spirit has inspired me to
initiate prayer groups and Bible studies, and
begin bridge building with local churches,
where families and clergy can be educated
about God's beloved gay and lesbian children.

I recently completed my long-delayed
dream of a seminary education, and now I want
with all my heart to be a faithful minister of the
gospel of Jesus Christ. As for my devout
Christian parents, they came to recognize that
my search and struggle as a lesbian had come
full circle, and the truth could no longer be hidden.

Hindsight has caused me to reflect on the
colossal accumulation of unnecessary suffering

in my life and the lives of those I love by my attempts to conform to mainstream Christian pressure. The same thing is happening to others. An antiquated and erroneous theology, nurtured by fear, confronts Christian gays and lesbians with unbearable exclusion, persecution, and rejection. No wonder some of them choose to conform, rather than risk the loss of family and church.

Also weighing on my heart is the realization that somewhere out there gay and lesbian people are tormented by the fear of accepting their God given identity. How many young men and women are agonizing in confusion, self-hatred, and spiritual torment? How many will remain trapped in dishonest marriages, drug and alcohol abuse, depression, and ultimately thoughts of suicide? How many times will this excruciating lesson have to be learned?

I heard recently that the Southern Baptists intend to begin a teaching marathon in local churches, emphasizing that homosexuality is unnatural and sinful, that homosexuals should be encouraged to change, and that heterosexual church members should help them. A few months ago, a New York conference for Catholic youth workers reported that it taught "the truth about homosexuality as sin," suggesting that "there is no such thing as a gay or lesbian teenager." The future promises more of these public conferences and false pronouncements. Many denominations are expelling local churches that proclaim themselves open and affirming to homosexuals. The only way we can be strong and resolute in resisting these pressures is to remain rooted and grounded in Jesus Christ. There we will harness the strength to exist as outcasts among outcasts.

The more I reflect on the humanness of Jesus, the more I realize how much He understands rejection, the heart wrenching loss of friends and family, and the risk of death -- all in exchange for the truth. The book of Proverbs declares; "...a true friend sticks closer than one's nearest kin." For me that friend is Jesus. Though tribulation accompanies my pursuit of honesty, my inner temple remains calm and restful in the One who has overcome the world.

I continue to search for other gay and lesbian people who share my convictions, but I am also getting used to life as the odd Christian out. The writer of the book of Hebrews reminds me that people of faith are "strangers and foreigners on the earth." But that isolation is buffered by the Apostle Paul, who assures me that "our citizenship is in heaven." In the meantime, I press onward, praying to find a place for myself in this world.

___ Ann Amideo

Ann is currently an Adjunct Professor in the Department of Health Professions and Family Studies at Hofstra University, in New York.

Ann conducts workshops for spiritual directors in the area of sexual orientation. She facilitates the local Catholic Parents of Gay/Lesbian Support Group, and also counsels individuals for guidance in their spiritual lives

I Am the Mother
of a Gay Son

I had my first suspicion that my son was gay when he was in senior high school. He developed a medical problem that the doctor diagnosed as stress. My son never dated but did attend the junior and senior high proms. After he graduated college, he went to Europe to study languages. He came home for the holidays and said he wanted to live in Germany. My gut feeling told me he wanted to conceal his sexual identity by living far away from his family and friends. At that time I owned my own hair salon and had many gay men and women working for me. They confided in me and told me that my son was gay.

At first I was in denial. After some time, I sat down with my son and asked him point blank if he was gay. With tears in his eyes he said to me, "Mom, do you know how I feel? I feel like a fish in a bowl looking out." I never forgot those words. I said to him, "You are my flesh and blood; I carried you inside of me for nine months. I've raised you and loved you dearly all these years. Did you think I could abandon you and not want or love you anymore because you are gay? Wrong! In fact, I love you more because you are special and God's gift to me. I will not deny the truth to anyone who asks if you are gay, nor do I want you to feel guilty or ashamed." I will always remember the look of relief on his face, as if a mountain had been lifted from his shoulders. His two sisters have accepted him with open arms and hugs. His health problem was cured, he finished his studies in foreign languages, and went on with his life.

My son joined a church open to gay people and I supported him all the way. I also became involved in the same church, in which we are both currently very active. I have dedicated many hours to the gay and lesbian community. I visit patients in the HIV ward in a nearby hospital. My son and I sing together in the church choir and much, much more. As a mother, whose love is the greatest in the world (besides the dear Lord our God), I cannot tolerate parents and families of gay people who discard their own children, brothers and sisters because of their ignorance and lack of knowledge about homosexuality. Homosexuals do not voluntarily choose to be gay. I pray more parents would become better educated before they judge their own children. Accept your children, brothers, sisters, friends and family as God created them. I am very proud of my son. He is an intelligent, kind, considerate and loving human being. I would not trade him for any heterosexual I know.

Jesus Loves Cowboys

My favorite TV shows were *The Cisco Kid,*
Hopalong Cassidy, Tom Mix, and *The Lone Ranger.*
During my childhood years I attended a strict
Catholic school. One morning Sister Mary Ignatius
gathered the class of children around her feet. She
decided that we were going to have an informal
discussion about what we wanted to be when we
grew up. Johnny wanted to be a fireman, Susie a
nurse, and Timmy a doctor. "Jamie, what do you
want to be when you grow up?" Without the
slightest hesitation I proudly announced, "a cowboy." She corrected me and told me that I wanted to be a "cowgirl." Instantly I envisioned Dale
Rogers riding a horse named "Buttercup." I could
not bear the thought of riding anything less than
Trigger or the Lone Ranger's Silver, and

I certainly couldn't imagine riding a horse with such a sissy name. So I battled it out with the nun in front of the rest of the class. We went at it, back and forth, until she finally realized she could not weaken my genuine desire to be a cowboy. She was frustrated and I won: a victorious moment indeed. I was six.

Approximately one year later, I remember running into the bathroom. The mirror was too high for me to view myself. I climbed up onto the sink and peered into the mirror, studying my face. I fantasized about becoming a boy and wondered when the change would occur. In my seven year old mind I resolved the frustration by telling myself I just had to be patient and wait, that it would eventually happen. Then I ran outside to play.

Three years later, in 1959, when my younger brother wanted to join the Little League, I spent hours teaching him to throw, catch, and hit a baseball. The day finally came when he was accepted on the local team. I stood behind the batting cage as he and the all boy team went to the other side of the field to practice. For the first time ever, I became acquainted with rejection. I knew I could play baseball better than most of the boys on that team, in fact, most of the boys in town. Except for the chatter on the other side of the field, it was a still and quiet morning in the park. I was happy for and proud of my brother, but incredibly frustrated that girls were not allowed to play baseball. I stood there for quite a while watching, on the verge of tears. I finally turned away and walked home alone.

I was the only girl playing with the boys in a rag-tag, neighborhood baseball game. I was in center field when Smitty got up to bat. He hit a pop-up fly to me, and seconds before it hit my glove, the sun's light pierced my vision. That was my first black eye. I ran home, put some ice on it and then ran back to the field to play until the sun went down. The next day at school, standing in line with my fifth grade class, my right eye was swollen and glowing with various colors. It certainly didn't match the dress I was forced to wear. The other students and teachers were staring at me. I was busting with pride. Everyone knew the black eye was because I was playing baseball with the boys. I was special that day; it was the high-light of my eleven years on earth.

Western Pennsylvania was the best place to grow up. I had friends, mostly boys. My younger brother and I were close. We'd walk along the rail-road tracks and cross over into the woods. Eventually we would make our way down to the river to play on a monkey rope near the Youghiogheny. We never went swimming in the river; even back then we knew it was polluted from the steel mills and various chemical compa-nies that were along the banks. When not playing ball or climbing trees, I was building forts. I would find old wood and anything that I could hammer through to make my building projects. My step-father was constantly searching for his hammer. The next day he would find it in the yard, with rust stains beginning to appear. He still brings it up. He would always chuckle at my "interests" and would usually accommodate me with the necessary tools. He had a wonderful pocket knife; the kind that had four or five different size blades. He taught me how to handle a knife by teaching me a game called "mumbly-peg." Using various techniques, I would sit in the yard for hours learning how to flip the knife into a circle of dirt. He carried that knife in his pocket everyday, and it was a great honor to be entrusted with it.

I was an athletic girl, but not tough unless I had to be. I was the oldest and the only fights I had were to defend my younger siblings. I was very protective regarding them. One time a boy harassed my younger sister on the way home from school by pushing her around. Infuriated that he was so relentless in his efforts to hurt her, I intervened and a fist fight ensued. It was quite a battle, and as she screamed for him to "leave her sister alone," I kept punching him until he ran away. Once I fought a girl two years older than me because she started to hit my younger brother. She towered over him. When I tried to stop her, she began to hit me. It was just a lot of slapping at first, then she began to kick me. That's when I began throwing punches. She finally realized I was not going to stop. She ran away, never to bother either of us again.

In 1960, I was 12 and the first girl in the neighborhood to deliver *The Daily News.* I had

150 customers. When I had to move to Florida two years later, I left behind 250 customers. I always had a pocketful of money and a nice bank account. I bought a used boy's bike from Western Auto with some of the money. The salesman tried to sell me a girl's bike. I wanted no part of that. How would I be able to ride double? I remember putting the boy's bike on layaway until I paid off the $25.

After my parents divorced, I had to give up my job, and my family moved to Florida. I experienced my first encounter with depression. I hated Miami. I hated palm tress. I missed Pennsylvania and was unhappy in my new school. The Cuban Missile Crisis was the frightening news of the day, and I felt extremely threatened being only 90 miles away from the Cuban shore. But as the crisis finally settled down, so did I. Eventually I acclimated to my new surroundings.

My mother certainly did her part to change me. She bought me dolls when I was a child, but much to her dismay, I insisted on footballs and baseballs. I had straight hair and forced permanents became a routine in my life, until I rebelled at 13. I also refused to attend church. I was raised Catholic until I was 12. I abhorred Catholic school and church. They terrified and confused me with their teachings and strictness. I had many night terrors about "hell" as a child. I would run through the house in the middle of the night in my sleep, trying to get away from the devil and the "flames of hell." By the time I attended a Methodist church, I was pretty confused about religion and God in general. I decided at 13 that if there was a God, he must be a monster. But mostly I thought that there was no God at all: a true teenage atheist. I would make fun of my friends if they tried to talk to me about God.

I was mostly interested in art and sports in high school. I loved to dance and also played guitar. I did date boys, but didn't like going steady or being serious. Most of the girls I knew seemed boy crazy and I couldn't understand why they wanted to get married when they were still in school. When I started community college I began dating a nice guy that I knew from high school. We became pretty serious. I liked him mostly because he wasn't superficial; we could talk. We had a lot of similar interests. We both owned classic 1955 Chevys. I loved working on my own car and it was great for him because he loved mechanics. The perfect couple we thought. We loved each other and made plans for marriage.

I picked an old church with ivy covered, coral rock walls, beautiful Spanish architecture, and grassy patios. It was in the art district of town. I was not a member, nor had I ever visited for a service. I had no feelings about God, and it didn't even occur to me that maybe I should pray before I made such a huge life decision. Marriage to me was a forever commitment. At twenty years old, I made a serious vow to myself that I would never get a divorce. After being raised with a number of divorces, I did not want to re-experience another one in my own life.

Less than six months into the marriage I knew I was gay. I thought it was weird that I had intense feelings for my girlfriends. I fought the feelings by dropping friends. I was very uncomfortable around other women and didn't know why I couldn't overcome this. It was very difficult trying to blend in and at the same time isolate myself. I didn't know anyone that was openly gay. It was the late 60's. Psychedelic music and hard rock and roll were in. I began smoking pot. At first it was fun, but after getting thoroughly addicted to it psychologically, I began to experience tremendous paranoia.

My boss at work told me about Jesus. I gave him a difficult time, as I continued to do so with others, but since he was my boss, I was a bit kinder. It was through his efforts to share the gospel that I finally accepted Jesus into my life. I began reading the Bible and also books by C.S. Lewis, Francis Schaeffer, and Hannah Whittall Smith. Yes, it changed everything. I experienced a complete change in direction. No more drinking parties and pot. No more constant vile language. I became kinder to people, and less cynical. I no longer had despairing feelings about the future and a disconnect with society, but instead, experienced hope. I was impressed with the changes and welcomed them. My husband also became a Christian. We had a child, a son. What an incredible blessing! The birth of my son was the first *big* prayer God answered. I prayed for a seven pound boy, with blue/green eyes and freckles. That is what I got, not an ounce over.

Everything seemed to be moving in a new direction. Everything, that is, except my continued discomfort being around women friends. Why was I uncomfortable? Because I was attracted to them. That never went away.

I began to pray quite intently that the discomfort and confusion regarding this issue would simply go away. After much prayer, there was no change. I became very depressed. I loved my husband and son. My husband and I communicated well, but I was not comfortable being with him intimately. But because of my vow to never divorce, I tried to be a wife to him in every way. Over the next *18 years* I sought help from marriage counselors, psychologists, psychiatrists, therapists, and pastors. I wanted to find peace regarding this relentless issue in my life. It never happened. For 18 years I confided in my husband that I had this problem. We discussed it at length, over and over throughout the years of our marriage. My depression was getting out of control. I would be depressed for two and three weeks at a time, and eventually even months at a time. We both continued to pray and tried not to let it interfere with what we did have, yet, it was becoming impossible to function.

The churches at the time were in full swing preaching against homosexuality. It was repeatedly taught how incredibly sinful it was to be gay. Yet I knew I was gay. I bought into the interpretation of Scripture that was being preached at the time. God enables us, and gives us the power to change, I was told. So, I was honest with God, and asked Him to "change me," so I would be "normal." I spent tons of money for counseling. No matter how hard and often I prayed, or what I tried, nothing changed. After over 18 years of marriage, I was facing an inevitable divorce, the one thing that I vowed against. We both made an honest, valiant effort to stay in a committed marriage, but it seemed that the relationship was doomed. After much prayer, repenting for being *different,* talking, emotion, agony, effort, time, and money, we sadly proceeded to divorce.

Sometimes people ask me if homosexuals try to change. I cannot speak for anyone else, but after exhausting innumerable resources over a period of *18 years* trying to change, it was obvious to me that I had to accept myself as a truly gay person. It was not a choice, I could not change, even though I wanted to. Is it possible that another few years would have made the difference? I don't think either one of us had much energy left to continue the battle. To stay in the marriage with this constant problem certainly wasn't fair to my husband either. We finally parted as friends, and still continue a friendship. His respect, support and encouragement have helped me tremendously, although ten years after the divorce, I was still beating myself up over it. I was distraught, and greatly concerned about my son. I was incredibly concerned about what God thought of me. Sooner or later, I had to come to terms with myself and God.

I became sadly aware of how difficult the gay "lifestyle" was. It was late in life for me to experience such a contrast. At the same time I was trying to understand the lack of acceptance by family, church, and society, I was also trying to balance life in an unfamiliar, underground world. It was extremely difficult, and it didn't help my self-worth to live a secretive life. My faith in God continued to help me through a maze of confusion. Even though I continued to have faith in Jesus, I struggled and made many mistakes. The journey has been a learning process and I have progressed spiritually and healed emotionally. I began to find peace through Christ when I finally began to accept myself for who I was. God has always been at peace with me, but He knew I needed to accept myself.

When asked if I die will I go to heaven, my answer is a resounding, unequivocal, "Yes!", not because I follow rules or try to be "good," but because I have faith in Christ alone. *~ Sola Fide ~*

_ _ _Jamie

Jamie loves the Lord Jesus and has been a believer for over 31 years. She has taught numerous Bible studies and workshops. She and her life partner, also a believer, have been together for over 8 years.

And Jamie has owned a horse for the past 23 years. Yes, Jesus does love cowboys!

Choosing the High Road

Hi, my name is Paul. I am a Christian who happens to be gay. Christian and gay, you ask? Yes, it's possible to be Christian and gay.

Let me tell you a little about myself. I grew up in the South, in a strict Catholic home. I was taught to believe that being gay was one of the evils that would definitely prevent you from receiving God's love. But, from my own experience, I can tell you that it is possible to be a Christian and gay. Without me even realizing it, God has blessed my life all along.

When I realized and accepted the fact that I was gay, I did what I was taught I had to do. That was to leave the Church and my faith behind, because God couldn't love a gay man. For a long time I was very unhappy. Something was missing from my life. I didn't know what that was, so I accepted it as my lot in life for "choosing to be gay."

In 1982, my life partner died. I was totally lost and all alone, or so I thought. I went for a walk one morning and ended up at the local church. As I was sitting there, the minister happened to notice me and came over to say hello; I think he knew that I needed someone to talk to. Did I ever need to talk to someone! I poured out my heart to this total stranger. When I was finished, he assured me that God still loved me and was walking right along beside me the whole time. I got down on my knees and prayed to God to guide me and tell me what to do. Within days I felt a sense of peace come over me. I knew that God heard my prayer and was telling me that it didn't matter that I was a gay man. If I would just love and trust in Him, He would take care of the rest. I was suddenly happy and at peace with myself.

I continued to worship the Lord. In 1990, I met my new life partner. He was not a Christian, but I decided that this was the person I wanted to spend my life with. Before we committed to each other, I made it very clear that I was a Christian and intended on staying a Christian, no matter what. In the beginning that was not a problem, but it eventually became a problem for him. He felt that I was spending too much time worshiping and loving the Lord Jesus and not enough time with him.

He told me that I had to make a choice between my faith and him. I loved this man dearly, but I also remembered the past, how unhappy and unfulfilled I was without Christ in my life. I chose to walk away from that relationship. As much as it hurt me to walk away, I have no regrets, because God has taken care of my every need. Again, He led me down the right path. All I had to do was love and trust Him and He did the rest.

If you are gay and feeling all alone, just remember that God does love you, gay or not. All you have to do is accept the Lord Jesus Christ into your heart and He will take care of everything else.

___ Paul

Paul is not an ordained minister, but in his spare time he ministers to the sick and dying in the hospitals. He prays with people with AIDs and reads the Bible to them, and often gives away Bibles. He has been a blessing and comfort for many who do not have visitors or family.

Liberty

"We can make a vision for the future where we are free to fulfill our human potential. This new framework will not support repression, hatred, exploitation, and isolation, but will be a human and beautiful framework, created in a community, bonded not by color, sex or class, but by love and the common goal for the liberation of mind, heart, and spirit." __ Merle Woo

The reason I am beginning my story with my vision is because, in recent years, I have experienced the pain of isolation, discrimination and rejection simply for the mere fact that I am gay. Once I was out, my family and friends suddenly found reasons to treat me differently. I had to face the reality that in this world we are going to experience isolation and prejudice due to people's fears and lack of understanding. It is my prayer that one day we can all come to the realization that God is love and that He loves us all the same, and that we are all beautifully made in His image.

I am a 39 year old woman. A woman who only became sexually aware at about 30 years old. I was blessed to be born into a wonderful Christian home. My homeland is the beautiful island of Cuba, a land I barely remember because I was six years old when my family left. Both of my parents are wonderful Christians, who taught me about God's love and faithfulness. My father is a preacher and my mother is a teacher and musician. I can truly say that in spite of the pressures of being a preacher's kid, it was a blessing to grow up in my home. Our home was always full of people, music, and a great deal of love. In early childhood, I learned that I had the freedom to talk to God in prayer. This has been one of the greatest gifts in my life.

My parents had two girls and two boys. I was the second child in my family. I remember having much more fun playing with my two younger brothers than with my sister. Playing outdoors was much more interesting than playing with dolls.

We left Cuba and moved to Europe, where my father would later get a post-graduate degree in theology. We left Cuba under difficult circumstances and were allowed to take only a few belongings. My memories from that experience are vague, but I do remember how my parents talked about God providing for all of our needs. As we relocated to a new country in the middle of winter, I recall my mother's face, full of joy, as we received boxes full of winter clothing donated by people from church. Many instances in our life as a family I remember my mother's words, "God will provide." That promise never failed.

We later moved to Central America. There I learned more about the God that my parents taught me to trust in. At a children's camp, I made the decision to have a personal relationship with Jesus. It was truly wonderful to be able to call Jesus my friend and Savior. As I grew up, I learned to trust Him with all my personal worries and feelings. As I prayed and read the Bible, I became more convinced of God's love and wanted so much to learn to be like Him. I could feel God's loving presence when I prayed. It was so wonderful to be able to trust in Him every day. My life was further enriched through my involvement with a very active youth group in my church. We worked with children in poor neighborhoods and helped youth that were involved with drugs. Even as young people, we were convinced that we were responsible for making a contribution in this world. I had a very supportive network of Christian friends and we encouraged each other in our walk with God. This was a very meaningful time in my life.

After finishing high school, I left the safety of my family and friends to study in the United States. I also left behind my best friend from church, who had become my first "real" boyfriend. In college, I found that learning English was difficult. Once again, my personal relationship with God and new Christian friends helped me to adjust to my new life. I was also very fortunate to go to a Christian college with very supportive teachers.

In college, I became aware that people have very different life experiences and that people have different ways of understanding their relationship with God. Growing up in a very close church environment made me feel secure but kept me somewhat unaware of the variety of experiences people have in life. The world of sex, alcohol, and drugs was foreign to me. It was just assumed that a girl from my background would not get involved with any of those three things. It was expected that you did not have sex until you were married. I continued dating my Central American boyfriend from church but rarely saw him, so I did not have a major problem keeping those expectations. In hindsight, I also remember that I only began dating him because he was my best friend and had pursued me for a long time.

After several years of long distance dating, my boyfriend and I decided to get married. However, we continued to live apart, since we were both finishing graduate work in different countries. I had great hopes and expectations for a good marriage, since we were good friends and both Christians. In spite of our friendship and common love for God, our sexual experience was a disaster from the beginning. We both realized early on that something was not right between us. I felt in my heart that although I loved my husband, I could not love him sexually. Our marriage ended in divorce after a couple of years. It was very painful to lose our friendship and experience the reality of a failed marriage.

This was the beginning of a painful journey. I started questioning God. I had prayed so much for His guidance in my life, I believed that He had let me down. I was disillusioned and confused. I was trying to follow God, yet my marriage ended in disaster. I could not understand why He had allowed me to experience such pain. I later realized that God does not prevent us from having painful experiences, but He gives us strength and comfort during those times. He never leaves us alone in the hour of darkness, as He shows up in the form of friends and loved ones to help out. Also, pain brings us closer to others with similar experiences.

When I was about 28 years old, my

youngest brother died tragically. His loss became so distressful to me that I went for therapy. In the process of therapy, I searched the depths of my soul. To my surprise, I realized that I was attracted to a woman.

This type of attraction was considered unacceptable to God by the church of my youth. Thus began another long, painful, but exciting journey. This was the beginning of new discoveries and a new relationship with God. Contrary to all the rules and values of my church, my feelings grew towards a young woman in this church. It was clear to her since childhood that she had an attraction to girls. We became romantically involved and I began to encounter pronounced grief. A battle was going on inside of me. I felt great love and joy, but I also felt pain, since I had been taught that being a homosexual was wrong. I tried to deny my feelings and prayed every day to be free of them. I searched my heart, and continued to go to therapy with a wonderful, loving therapist, who was very gentle during my process of discovery. I believe this particular therapist was sent by God because of her gentle nature and lessons on unconditional love.

I struggled for some time, but finally came to realize that in the midst of my confusion, God was still there, right beside me. I asked for wisdom, peace, and understanding. My prayers were answered. He gave me peace. I cannot fully explain how it happened, but I finally felt God's love and understanding. I accepted myself as I was and allowed myself to continue this same-sex relationship. I found that it was possible for two women to love each other and also experience God's love.

After I came out to my parents and a couple of close friends, they severed their relationships with me. Friends that I had supported and encouraged in the past rejected me and became critical and judgmental of me. This actually brought me closer to God, my constant companion. It also helped me to bond with other friends who were unconditional. My parents and previous Christian friends do not understand that the God of my youth is the same God that gave me peace as I came to grips with my sexuality.

It does not matter whether we love a man or a woman. What matters is that God created us, that He loves each one of us in a special way, and that we are here to learn to love each other as He loves us: *unconditionally!*

May the God that gave me peace give you peace in your journey.

___Beate

Beate is a social worker for the public school system in South Florida. Through GLSEN (Gay, Lesbian, Straight Education Network), she gives presentations that increase people's awareness of the issues that affect the gay youth.

Beate is also a singer, guitarist, and songwriter. She uses her talent and love for the Lord to minister to the elderly in local nursing homes.

Small Steps First

I feel like I wandered in the desert, like Moses, for 40 years. Two months before my 40th birthday, God had had enough of my wandering and unbelief. He came after me.

At age 27, my life started to really go downhill. I chose the path of drugs, alcohol and very loose morals, for approximately 8 years. I was trying to kill the pain of losing the love of my life. I was trying to escape from the incredible loneliness and desperately trying to fill the void. The more I tried to medicate and drink away the pain, the worse it became. I didn't realize that the things I was doing to myself were actually making it worse. I was in a black hole and could not escape, no matter how hard I tried. I had only one prayer for years; "God, if you really exist, please take away the pain, just let me be happy."

I never prayed any other prayer and was never thankful for anything in that darkness. I didn't see anything to be thankful for.

I think I always believed in a Higher Power, but did I believe in Jesus or the Bible? Why should I? Even the Jews (one of which Jesus was supposed to be), the majority of His own people, did not believe He was the Son of God. Why should I believe anything written in the Bible? I thought it was written by ordinary men who were trying to manipulate and control others.

At 39, I found myself questioning more and more and starting to get into the New Age thing. I was learning about meditation and asked a friend about her New Age church. Actually, I couldn't stand the thought of organized religions. I felt that they were a bunch of hypocrites. Yet, I knew that the universe didn't randomly happen, and that there had to be a Creator. But, New Age or not, I was not going to attend a church of any kind. Besides, the weekends were mine and I planned on sleeping until noon on my days off.

One particular Sunday something woke me up early, nine a.m. in fact. I was raring to go, very unusual for me. I got dressed and drove to the Unity church. I drove, but felt as though I was "driven." I sat outside and watched the people go in. "What am I doing here? I don't want to go in there, sit by myself and participate in who knows what." But inside I went. It was okay and I met some nice people. I was hugged coming and going, which made me feel very uncomfortable. It was a nice service that included a guided meditation. We were told what to picture in our minds. I didn't really think that was so bad. So I went back the following week.

The next week the pastor led everyone in another guided meditation. I was very relaxed, mind empty, focusing on his words. I will pause here to say that I had never experienced visions or hallucinations before, nor do I now. But, with all my heart, I believe I had a vision on that day. I saw Jesus standing on the right hand side of God. He spoke to me and said, "I am the way, and the truth, and the life. No one comes to the Father except through Me." This very real experience was not part of the guided meditation. God wanted me to know that if I intended to be saved, I had to believe in His Son. It was the only way.

What did God look like in my vision? A brilliant, white light, not without form, situated on a throne. Jesus was in human form and His face was scarred. That is all I can remember.

My life did not change immediately, but from that day forward, I believed and accepted that Jesus was the Son of God. I felt that I had been given a very rare and precious gift. God must have wanted me badly, and known I would have continued rationalizing until the day I died. He let Jesus speak to me. Thank you Lord, for saving my soul.

I was a baby Christian then. I was led from the New Age thing to the Metropolitan Community Church. This denomination welcomes gay people. I was ready to study the Bible and let everyone know that the Bible was written by ordinary men and was mostly untrue...except, of course, that Jesus was real. But it just didn't happen that way. Instead, I found myself absorbing the words in the Bible like a very thirsty person in the middle of the desert. I soon believed that everything in the Bible, even the miracles, were all true. The Bible became alive to me.

I pray many different prayers now, and I am no longer stuck in that lonely, black hole, which was my hell on earth. It took me 40 years to start listening to God and to quit being stubborn. God has brought many wonderful people into my life and I have made many good friends. Most of my friends are Christians.

God wanted me, and He wants you too. He loves us all. Listen to Him. Pray, meditate, read the Bible. Believing in Jesus will change your life (as it did mine); it only takes faith. Remember, sometimes you first have to take small steps to eventually discover "the Way."

Who Can Be Against Me?

"He hath shewed thee O man, what is good; and what
doth the Lord require of thee, but to do justly, and to
love mercy, and to walk humbly with thy God."
Micah 6:8 (KJV)

My name is Sandy and this is just part of my story. I was raised in the Assembly of God Church. I always had a knowledge of God, but not the God I know today. I heard the Bible verse above over and over again in church, but never really understood its meaning until recently.

My parents were both alcoholics. My mother abandoned our family when I was five, leaving my father to raise me and my three siblings. During my childhood, I was molested by my father and older brother. When I told my pastor about this, he simply replied that he was sick of my family and all our problems.

As far back as I can remember, I was a tomboy and attracted to the same sex. I was raised in a fundamental church, which taught that it was a sin to be homosexual. I would sit at the altar in the church, night after night, crying at times for hours. I felt guilty about my sexuality and longed for someone I could trust and talk to. But there was no one and I kept those feelings inside. Throughout my teen years I struggled mercilessly over my thoughts and how bad a person I was to think in such a way. How could God love me with the feelings I had?

By the time I was 15, I had to get away and left home. Tragedy upon tragedy came along. A close friend committed suicide in front of me. There was incest and numerous rapes in my family. My stepsister was kidnapped, raped and murdered. An uncle, whom I loved and respected, died. I went over the edge and tried to kill myself with a drug overdose. I spent six months in a psychiatric ward. Upon release, I found it hard to cope. I had to learn to adjust, but what was I to do with my homosexual proclivity? This had to be addressed but I still had nowhere to turn.

Over and over I was told that I had to live a certain way in order to be loved by God. After trying so hard to be what others said I should, knowing that I could not, I walked away from the Lord. I lived on the streets for months at a time and experimented with every imaginable type of drug to escape reality.

My first marriage was a disaster from the beginning. I agreed to marry this man while I was high on cocaine. He said he would change the way I felt about women. A year later my son was born. I tried so hard to be committed to my husband, who was also a substance abuser, but failed and had many affairs with women. I was depressed and tried numerous times to kill myself.

My second marriage was to an older man who appeared to love me and my son. Initially, he treated us well. After we married he physically abused me. My depression got worse and I continued to pursue one night stands at the bars. Finally, after more abuse, I left my second husband.

I joined the Army, thinking it would be good to get a college education while serving. When I enlisted, there was talk about war in the Persian Gulf and I knew I would probably end up there. Sure enough, as soon as I finished my training I was on a plane to Saudi Arabia.

I was trained as a truck driver. My squad leader told me that I would be joining a convoy into Iraq. I was already out in the desert when I was told I would be burying bodies. I was shocked. That was not part of my job description, but orders were orders. Two men in my squad were sent with a refrigerator truck to pick up American casualties, while the other four, including myself, went to collect the Iraqi dead.

We drove along the road from Kuwait to Basra, known as the "highway of death." When we got into Iraq there were bodies everywhere. I had never seen so many dead people at one time. It was gruesome: burned bodies in vehicles and even women holding babies, all dead. At first we were given rubber gloves, but when we ran out we used our bare hands. We wore the same body suits for four weeks. Sometimes it was so hot we stripped to our shorts and T-shirts.

One day, in the middle of the desert, while taking a truck to another unit with a fellow soldier, he stopped the truck and raped me. When I got back to the base, I told my squad leader what happened. He did nothing. I wrote a statement of charges against my attacker, but no one ever did anything about it. In the end, I was told that the burden of proof was on me. If the soldier accused me of engaging in voluntary sexual behavior, then I, still married, would be charged with adultery.

March 20, 1991, I returned to the United States. The war was over but my own battle had just begun. I became very sick. I began vomiting and developed strange rashes all over my body and lumps on my arms and legs. When I first heard the term "Gulf War Syndrome," I realized I wasn't alone. I was sent from hospital to hospital and underwent numerous tests. I was told it was stress. I was also experiencing nightmares and flashbacks. Amidst my anger and frustration, I attempted suicide again and ended up back in a psychiatric ward.

I was given a general discharge from the military. As my physical condition got worse and worse, I decided I wanted to die with dignity. I wrote to Dr. Kevorkian. His assistants replied and said they were going to discuss it with me. However, at that time Dr. Kevorkian himself was going to trial, so nothing came of it.

While still on active duty in the Army, I had a two year, loving relationship with a woman. I thought I had finally come to believe that God loved me as I was and I shared that with her. I told her it was okay to be Christian and gay, but I really didn't believe it myself. Eventually, I ended the relationship and apologized to her for leading her astray.

I got involved with a well known Christian ex-gay ministry. For three years, I tried so hard to do the things I was told would make me acceptable to God. They told me to dress like a lady. I bought a whole new wardrobe and began wearing dresses, skirts, nylons, purses and pretty little shoes. But there was no change inside of me. They told me I did not have enough faith in God to heal me from this sin. But I believed I did.

I tried to find a church that could help me. But each time I found a reason to leave. A longtime friend and mentor knew my confusion. I am sure she spent a lot of time over the years praying for me. She tried to help me understand God's grace. But all I saw was hypocrisy. I spent a lot of time in a spiritual wasteland.

My longtime friend continued to talk to me about God's grace. *Finally,* I realized who I was in Christ: a believer, a daughter, a mother, who just happened to be gay. I accepted myself as I really was. God had changed my life for good. I no longer went to the bars looking for someone to fulfill my needs. I relied upon God. I realized that if the Lord wanted me to have a partner, He would provide one.

I have become a more loving person. The Bible states, "For God so loved the world that He gave His only begotten son, that *whosoever* believes in Him, shall have everlasting life." (KJV, emphasis added). This means that anyone who comes to the Lord Jesus, asking for His forgiveness and mercy, is made right with God. The turmoil that was inside me has finally broken loose. Although I have become physically disabled by the Gulf War Syndrome, I am a much stronger person. I have learned to love others with the love that Jesus has for us. I have finally come to know peace, a peace that only the Lord can give.

There were so many times in my life when I felt confused and hopeless and wanted to throw in the towel. But, through the love of Jesus Christ, I no longer have those despairing feelings. I want to live my life to its fullest, in His service, and be a light for others to see the love of God. The God I was searching for has always been there, I just needed to tune into Him and His love, and believe it was real. I am no longer concerned if others reject me for who I am. I do not seek acceptance from others as I once did in the past. I know now that I have been accepted by God through the precious blood of Jesus Christ. If God is for me, who can be against me?

_____ Sandy

Since writing this testimony, Sandy lost her 20 year old son to a serious illness on February 7, 2002. This was her only son, yet God has given her peace in the midst of this difficult loss. Her faith in God has remained intact. She continues to be an active Gulf War veteran advocate. She is now 40 years old, and her health continues to present problems. She takes daily pain medications and uses a walker or wheelchair to get around. She receives disability, but volunteers at the library in her community, where she is especially blessed to be involved with the children's reading program.

Hate Is Not a Family Value

Thanksgiving 2001, I was invited to visit friends in a small town in North Florida. The family included a young daughter, Judy, who was going to have a birthday celebration while I was there. Judy wanted to have her hair cut professionally, and I told her I would gladly pay for that as a present from me. Her mother made an appointment at a nearby salon.

Judy's two friends wanted to go along. When we arrived at the salon we were all greeted by a man who said he could take Judy next. I felt good about him immediately. He seemed very patient with the teenagers and I sensed Judy would feel at ease and happy with him.

While Judy was getting her hair cut, I waited in the sitting area with her two teenage friends. The girls were being silly. All of a sudden they shrieked and ran to the storefront window. Passing by was a boy they knew from school. They said he was gay.

They also mentioned how they hated gay people. They said gay people were going to hell. "How could anyone be gay?" they asked. They continued for a brief time to verbally put the boy down. They were quite loud and unaware that the hairdresser was also listening. I became embarrassed by their open disdain and verbal insults. When we first arrived I sensed that the hairdresser himself might be gay. I was concerned about his feelings over this outburst of hatred in his own store.

I told them that I had some wonderful gay friends. They asked me, "Why?" I told them that everyone needs friends. The hairdresser, upon overhearing me, motioned for me to come over, while he continued to cut Judy's hair. He wanted to know what church we all went to. The teenagers told him of the local church they attended. I told him that I was from out of town, and that I was looking for a church in my hometown where I felt I could fit in. He said he was having trouble finding one to fit into also.

I am not gay, but I do know how difficult it is for my gay friends to find a place of worship. I felt very bad for this man and realized how difficult it must be for him. The girls were completely oblivious to the fact that he was gay. Had they realized, they would not have made such a scene in front of him.

Judy and her friends were thrilled with the haircut. In fact, we all made a great fuss and told the hairdresser what a great job he did. We were piling into the van to make our way home and, once again, the gay controversy came up. I told them that I thought the man who cut Judy's hair was also gay. Their mouths dropped open. I'm sure some of their reaction was embarrassment over how cruel they had been. Yet, they still couldn't understand how I could accept gay people. They thought that if they were friends with someone gay at school, then everyone would think that they were also gay. I mentioned the boy that passed by the store. "How do you think he must feel with everyone putting him down and calling him names? What an awful thing to have to live everyday with that kind of abuse," I said. They sat in guilty silence. The evening before, at a sleep over, the same young ladies had an argument, calling each other hurtful names. I reminded them of that incident and asked them how that made them feel. They said, "Sad." I told them that gay people get their feelings hurt every day. Sometimes their families even reject them and churches preach against them. That is where we find comfort and love, but gay people only find more rejection. I reminded them that God loves everyone and wants us to love one another.

After much thought, Judy said she was going to try to befriend the gay boy at school. She was very troubled by her attitude and the behavior of her two friends, and realized that it needed to change. I hope her two friends are joining her in accepting those that are different.

___ Katie

Katie, a Christian for over 30 years, has been active in children's ministries in various churches, and is an award-winning Girl Scout leader. Katie adopted a mentally and physically challenged daughter, who recently passed away. She has also worked in a temporary foster care ministry for children who have lost their parents due to drugs, imprisonment, and death. Katie is a very accepting and loving Christian heterosexual who has embraced God's unconditional love for His entire creation.

America, America

My name is Isabel. I was born in South America and came to the United States ten years ago looking for a bright future and to escape from myself. Little did I know that God had different plans for me. My father used to tell my sister and me that we were not here by coincidence or mistake. "You are here," he would say, "because your mother and I wanted you." He would add, "because we loved you even before you were born." He was not aware that he was speaking words from the Bible. We were not Bible readers; we were not raised in the Church. We were Catholic, but that was just a name; we didn't really know what that meant.

I was leading a life of quiet desperation, going through the motions, always thinking, "Is this all there is?" I was unhappy with myself and depressed. My life had no direction. I had my share of unhealthy relationships that never culminated in a committed, loving union. How could they? I thought I was living as my true self, but in reality, I was living as I thought I was supposed to, according to others. Needless to say, I was lost. God was not part of my life so I was left to myself, to my all too powerful, independent self! Independence, apart from God, had taken me to a place of misery and unfulfillment. I couldn't see it because I didn't know any different. As one of my mentors used to say, "People don't know what they don't know." But it was not yet my time.

In spite of myself, God was working in my life, though I was not aware of it. It was He who instilled in me a skill for languages that led me to study English from an early age. When I was ten years old, I used to dream that I was a famous singer, singing in English.

I went through all the stages of education and graduated as an English-Spanish translator. I took a job as a bilingual secretary in an important company. Slowly my death began. It was a dead-end job, but a bad economic situation left me with no option but to stay. My dreams of having my own translation business faded and I was left with just the daily struggle to survive. I lost hope, enthusiasm, and faith in myself. I would not turn to God, but in retrospect, He showed up anyway, on time as always.

In 1987, I met a person from London in the most "coincidental" way. It was a Thursday and I was at home because I was sick. Otherwise, I would have been at work and would have never met this man. He came with a relative of mine, both on a business trip. They visited for the afternoon and he was very impressed with my fluency in English. He asked me if I had ever thought of going to the United States. I replied that ever since I visited there, when I was 15 years old, I wanted to live in America.

Two years later I received a phone call from this same gentleman. He asked me if I was really serious about going to America. I said definitely yes. He had established a business in Florida and had a job there for me. He said he would take all the legal steps to obtain a residence visa for me so I would be able to work legally. I was in shock; I could not believe my ears. It was a dream come true! But another 2 1/2 years had to elapse before my visa was ready for me to emigrate.

I arrived in Miami in 1992. I had a job, a furnished apartment, and a promising future. I cannot describe the joy, excitement, and zest for life that I experienced when I arrived. Everything was first class. There was cleanliness, peace, freedom, possibilities, money, order, a working legal system, endless summer and sunshine, Hurricane Andrew, lush vegetation, alligators, affordable cars, and a strong democracy. What a contrast from what I had always known! I was living a dream; I was living in America, the best country in the world! It was then that I started to think that God must have had something to do with this. Obviously, I hadn't done anything to create this other than having a desire to come here. I started to give God thanks and started to ponder what He wanted me to do here besides living a happy life for myself. I wanted to give my family some of the comforts and abundance that I enjoyed here. So I started my own business in addition to my original job.

I enjoyed the freedom and challenge of making my own decisions, but had to adjust to living by myself, a person that I hardly knew. With the happiness came questions about myself. I realized that I did not like myself, and became depressed. I didn't know how or what to change; I needed help. Falling deep into depression, old suicidal feelings came back. Fortunately, a dear childhood friend came to visit me and encouraged me to look for a psychotherapist. I searched and found the right one.

The therapist helped me uncover and remove layers of self-destructive opinions about myself. This enabled me to enjoy, to care for, and to love myself. One day she pointed out that it was time for me to look for a spiritual connection. She gave me a list of three churches to consider. I chose the MCC Sunshine Cathedral and attended for some time. It was a beautiful experience at first: the music, the choir, the little white lights hanging from the ceiling. It was also comforting to feel the love of God and the kindness of the people. The Catholic service took me back in time to when I was little and went to the church in my neighborhood. The difference was that now God was becoming real to me. Surrounded by a hundred people, I cherished every Sunday service, especially the prayers and communion. Although the concept of God was still far reaching, I began to trust Him.

The next church I attended was the Body of Christ Church, another enlightening experience. I had never been to a Protestant service. It was different and I enjoyed it and the people. Emphasis was placed on reading the Bible, which I had never read. I saw this as a wonderful opportunity to learn. There were several Bible studies during the week. I chose one and my spiritual path started to change. I made wonderful friends, including the teachers, with whom I now share an enriching personal friendship. I discovered the real God who is present everyday of my life, the God who sent His Son to die on the cross so that I can have everlasting life. I learned that God loves me unconditionally and that He sees Jesus when He sees me. This is grace, a gift from God to show me that He is at peace with me. Yet, there was one more decisive moment to come on my spiritual path.

One Sunday morning, in March 1998, I gave my life to Jesus Christ in this little storefront church. At the end of the pastor's sermon we all bowed our heads. He said that anyone who was not sure that Jesus Christ was in his or her life should raise a hand and he would pray. I raised my hand. Immediately I felt chills throughout my body, a struggling in my throat, and tears running down my face, while *Amazing Grace* was playing softly. At that moment I knew I had started on my path back home: not my home country, but my true home. I was at peace with God.

I had a voracious desire to learn more about God, His character and His Word. My Bible teachers facilitated this. The blessing of learning the Bible with these particular teachers was another surprise from God. I met them by "coincidence." They taught how to study the Bible without denominational bias. This has really made a difference in the way I view God and His message. I now know that

God is so much bigger than what most think. I learned to love the Jewish people and realized that God is not finished with them. I learned that the Law of Moses was never given to me, as a Gentile, and I began to understand what my role as a believer is in this age of grace. I have a new understanding of myself, others, the world, death, and after death. Ultimately, I know where we will all be when God achieves His plan for all of His creation.

Today, still suffering from the ripples of September 11th, 2001, I remain confident, because I know, without a shadow of a doubt, that God is in control. I like that! I prefer that! Knowing God, I believe He will never abandon me. Even in the most difficult times, He is with me. There are no coincidences. "I can do all things through Christ who strengthens me."

Being a believer in Christ, I am not problem free, but able to rise above the problem and trust God. It is the most reassuring feeling, the most comforting peace. It is "the peace that surpasses all understanding." It is this same peace that I now leave with you. God bless you.

___ Isabel

What Is a Nice Jewish Doctor Doing in a Book Like This?

I was not abused. I was not unloved or rejected by family. I was not addicted to drugs or alcohol. I was not raised poor. I was not without relatively good health. I was not without direction or advanced education.

Actually, I was a 29 year old woman, from a nice, well-off, traditional Jewish family. I had just finished 12 years of college, medical school, and residency and had a bright future ahead of me. So how then was it possible that one day I found myself with several bottles of pills, wanting desperately to end my emotional and psychological pain, to leave this world and commit suicide? How could this be and why am I now willing and able to write about it 11 years later, the same person yet completely new?

I was divorced and had a subsequent failed relationship. But that was not enough to have taken all the life out of me. It was much bigger than that, beyond my own life. Despite all that I had, the sadness, hatred, and cruelty in the world overwhelmed me. No matter what I did, what I achieved, what I bought, who I had a relationship with, or where I traveled, nothing really mattered. My every thought ended in "so what." I saw no purpose to life, with all its pain and suffering, or hope for the world's future. I did not want to be part of it anymore.

Knowing the pain I would have caused my family, I decided not to take the pills. But something was desperately missing. Something so great that, despite all I had, I was in a very deep clinical depression, always thinking about suicide. I searched for answers: therapists, psychiatrists, psychologists, antidepressants, sports, travel, hiking, nature, religion, friends and family. All I ever asked for was to be shown one thing that gave me hope. Not one person or thing offered me a solution: not even close. I lived just going through the motions.

About four years later, still depressed, although somewhat less, I asked a new acquaintance,

"How do you deal with all the adversity?" She answered, "I pray about it." I had never heard anyone say that before with such honesty and sincerity. Doubtful, yet inquisitive, I asked her, "Are you serious?" "Yes," she said, "I have a lot of faith in God and talk to Him about everything." "And that really works for you?" I asked. "Yes," she answered.

Those four words, "I pray about it," stuck in my mind. I was raised in a very secular environment. The only prayers I ever heard were in temple or at holiday meals, mostly in Hebrew, recited from the prayer books. When she actually said a prayer with me, a short, simple, from the heart, unrehearsed, prayer in English, I was extremely moved. No one had ever prayed with me like that before. Could it be so simple? I wanted to know more about this. We talked more and more. She told me she was a Christian and explained to me what that really meant. It was her faith in God and Jesus Christ that gave her peace and hope.

Well that was just great. But I am Jewish. Jews cannot believe in Jesus...can they? Anyway, although I had never completely stopped believing in God, I had totally given up on religion. All I saw from religion was separation, hatred, murder and war. But something deep inside was nudging me; go ahead, learn more about this before you reject it.

She gave me a Bible. I could not even open it to the New Testament without feeling like I was betraying my family and Jewish community. So I first read a book called *Your God Is Too Small,* by J.B. Phillips. It reset and greatly expanded my views of God and the possibility that Jesus could be the Jewish Messiah. I was then able to open the New Testament. I started reading the Gospel of Matthew. There it was, right on the first page! Jesus was a Jew, a descendant of Abraham, Isaac, and Jacob. He was raised as a Jew and followed the Law of Moses, the Torah. He was one of *us* not *them.* Not only was he one of us but He was sent by God *for* us, "to the lost sheep of the house of *Israel.*" The more I read, especially all the Old Testament prophecies about the coming Messiah that Jesus fulfilled, the more convinced I was that Jesus was the Jewish Messiah.

My mind was bombarded with questions. Why should I believe the Bible is the Word of God and not just another book written by men? How could all the rabbis be wrong about Jesus? Would I no longer be a Jew if I believed? Could I survive giving up this extremely important identity and risk being rejected by my fellow Jews? This would be the worst thing I could tell my family, even worse than being gay. What about all the persecution and atrocities committed against the Jews throughout history in the name of Christ? What about the Holocaust and all the suffering in the world?

Then I read the following words spoken by Jesus: "Come to me, all you that are weary and are carrying heavy burdens, and I will give you rest." It was as if He was sitting right next to me. I began to feel the weight of the world lifting from my shoulders and I began to see light at the end of the tunnel. I knew it was the truth. Jesus *is* the Jewish Messiah, and it was natural and desired by God for me to believe. I was no longer depressed and had true hope for the very first time.

I wanted to know more and more. I decided to put my pre-existing beliefs, which were based on traditions and religious teachings, on a shelf and start fresh, like a blackboard wiped clean, ready to receive new information without bias. I studied the Scriptures, both Old and New Testaments, as much as I could and was blessed with an outstanding mentor, who guided me with great insight and care. She gave me a book called *The Christian's Secret of a Happy Life*, by Hannah Whitall Smith. This book explained to me how to implement my faith and trust in God everyday in order to live a life of peace, joy and thanksgiving, under any circumstance.

It is now eight years later. I have learned so much I could not possibly tell it all in this story. Even with all my education, nothing has ever been as interesting and inspiring as the Bible. My scientific background has shown me that it takes more faith not to believe in God and creation than to believe. My Jewish issues and other questions, including whether or not the Bible is the Word of God, have been satisfactorily answered. According to God, I will always be a Jew, no matter what I believe. I have not "converted" or given up my belief in the one true God of Israel. I have simply accepted the full blessings God has given to all people through His Son, the Messiah. The more I learn, the more my faith grows and the bigger, more awesome, and loving God becomes. Now that I understand God's character and grace, and His glorious plan for all mankind and the universe, even when questions remain unanswered, I can completely trust in Him and know that He is in control.

My peace has come not through religion, which is man-made, but through a personal relationship with God through faith in His Son Yeshua (Hebrew for Jesus). He Himself said it so simply: "Peace I leave with you; my peace I give to you." As a homosexual, I know that my faith is real and acceptable to God. I have seriously studied the Bible verses used to condemn homosexuality. In their proper context and translation, they do not condemn same-sex, loving, and monogamous relationships. It is God's grace alone, through faith, which has brought me into a right relationship with Him. More importantly, no one can judge or take away my faith in Yeshua.

God has blessed me with a loving, devoted partner, also a believer, and a beautiful relationship that I never thought was possible. God is our top priority and focus. It was only after I accepted God's unconditional love and allowed His Spirit to fill my heart that I could truly give and receive the same type of love, with complete trust, to another.

As if being Jewish and homosexual wasn't enough to keep me from believing in Jesus, my faith took on a serious test when my physical suffering began. I developed a syndrome of constant headache, body pain, fatigue and a host of other symptoms, labeled fibromyalgia, over the last few years. Despite the innumerable therapies I have tried, I continue to get worse, and have found nothing which relieves the headache or other symptoms. I know something is causing my symptoms, and although I have not found it yet, I will continue to search for the cause and proper treatment. I had to give up my job and possibly my career, which I worked so hard and long to achieve. I cannot do most things which were part of my life, even things as simple as talking, without increasing the pain and fatigue. My life, as I knew it, has been taken from me.

I can't imagine how awful it would be to live with my condition without faith, hope and trust in the Lord. It would have all been viewed as useless pain and suffering. I am forever grateful to God for the faith He has given me. I am finally resting on a solid foundation. It is untouched by my changing emotions and desires, and brings peace and rest for my soul.

You see, it's all about contrast. How do we know "good" if we have never known "bad"? I will surely appreciate the wonders of heaven. I know in *all* things God is molding me and bringing me into His perfect will. That is where I want to be.

So, can a Jew, with a condition of chronic pain and fatigue, who is a homosexual, have faith in God, Jesus and the Bible, and receive all the spiritual blessings, including peace, love and hope, that come with this faith? My answer is absolutely *yes!* No matter who we are, or what we have accomplished, God has created us with a place in our hearts that only He can fill. Wipe the slate clean and give yourself the opportunity to start fresh and discover the truth. God has done it all for us; we simply have to receive His gift and believe. It seems so complex, yet is really so very simple.

"Differently-Abled"

*"I can do all things through Christ
who strengthens me."*
Phillipians 4:13 (KJV)

I am the oldest of six siblings and grew up in a very poor family. My father was a construction worker and my mother a housewife.

I began working when I was nine. My first job was delivering newspapers. As I walked the streets of a mid-western college town every afternoon, I threw papers from a heavy bag that dragged on the ground. I used to pass a large university and often told myself that one day I would go to that big school and find out what makes little girls hurt inside.

There are two things that I have always known about myself. First, I am a tomboy. I always liked the outdoors and hard physical work, and I prefer jeans to dresses. The second thing is that I have always pursued God. Throughout my childhood I was fascinated by God and church. I would bum a ride to church with whomever would take me.

When I was a year old, I was left with an aunt and uncle while my mother went to the hospital to have her second child. I was literally dropped off on their doorstep. I do remember this, even though child development studies state that this cannot be so. I remember being frightened, feeling abandoned and seeking comfort. This is my first memory of experiencing God. I felt God's presence. God was a friend to a scared little girl.

During my early childhood, my family moved often. When I was seven, we lived in a housing project. A bus from the Baptist church would come through the project and pick up neighborhood kids for church. I was first in line every Sunday to get on the bus so I could learn about Jesus.

The pastor held a contest that year. The person to bring the most visitors to the Easter service would win a Bible. I was so excited. I went door to door inviting people to church. Sure enough, I won that Bible. It was my first one. I used if for the next 15 years until I wore it out.

During my school years, I attended churches of various denominations. I went to Catholic Sunday school and mass with my cousins. I went to a Methodist church with my grandmother, an Episcopal church with her brother, a Baptist church with an aunt. I attended a Christian Missionary Alliance church with some neighbors. I went to see a televangelist with one of my mother's friends, and to a Pentecostal church with another of my mother's friends. Denominations did not matter to me. I wanted to be near God and I felt near God when I was in church.

At 12, I answered an altar call at a Christian Missionary Alliance summer camp and accepted Jesus Christ as my Lord and Savior. Two things I knew for certain. I was saved and I was called by God to the ministry. I became very active in the youth group in our local Christian Missionary Alliance church.

Throughout junior high and high school, I had crushes on female teachers, female movie stars, and other teenage girls. I didn't act on the crushes and I certainly did not talk to anyone about them.

When I was 18, I married a farm boy who lived up the road from me. Eleven months later, I had my daughter (my only child). I played the role of submissive wife and mother really well for about eight years, until I could no longer stand the abuse. My husband abused me physically, emotionally, and sexually. When I realized that he was also abusing my daughter, I finally left him. My daughter and I escaped to a battered women's shelter.

It was there that I realized the pattern of abuse that had been in my life. My father and grandfather were also very abusive. My past reeked with physical, sexual, and emotional abuse by men whom I was supposed to trust. My mother was also very abusive to me, so all I knew was abuse and abusive atmospheres. I was a victim and I had attracted a perpetrator.

My daughter and I were so imprisoned with my first husband that we were literally locked up. He built a house way back in the woods and put a chain across the driveway to lock us in and lock the world out. I worked third shift (11 p.m. to 7 a.m.) at a factory. My husband locked the gate when I got home and did not unlock it until I went back to work.

Soon after I left my first husband, I married an older man on a rebound. I thought he was going to take care of us. He was a heavy drinker and I soon became a heavy drinker as well. I drank daily for about eight years and became an out of control alcoholic.

I was living in a brand new $150,000 plus home, driving a Cadillac, selling real estate, and attending that large university that I used to pass everyday when I was a paper girl. Then, while hanging siding on a house that my husband and I were building, I fell off a ladder, broke my leg, and was put in a cast from my toes to my butt. I was left alone, bedridden, while my husband was at work (teaching) and my daughter at school. Suddenly I was alone with "me," and it was frightening. It appeared as though I had it all, but I felt so empty. I did not know who I was, what I wanted, or where I belonged. This was the beginning of a nightmare that ended with peace.

Within six months I realized that I was an

absentee mom, an alcoholic, a backslidden Christian, a survivor of sexual abuse, and a lesbian. I shared my discoveries with my husband who handled it exceptionally well. I peacefully moved out of our home to a nearby city.

For the next five years I attended AA meetings, went for counseling, and began dating women. I experienced times of deep depression and spent time in the stress management ward of a hospital. I struggled with self-esteem, my sexuality, and Christianity.

I called a pastor in a local gay affirming church. She told me that God loves me and He made me to be the person I am. I visited a pastor at another gay affirming church who shared Scripture with me and assured me that Jesus saves "whosoever" believes in Him. I prayed about my spirituality and sexuality issues and soon began to have a relationship with Jesus again. Meanwhile, I was dealing with another situation. The leg that had broken was now about to be amputated.

A few months after I moved to the city, while prying an aluminum lid off a soda bottle with a serrated knife, I cut my left pointer finger so badly that it took a five hour operation to save it. Several weeks later, I went for a post-op checkup and I was limping. The doctor asked me why I was limping and I told him that I had broken my leg several months ago, had twisted it the night before, and it was hurting. The doctor took an x-ray of my leg and told me that I needed to have a tibial rod inserted. This surgery involved pulling the leg away from the knee and placing a rod down through the weight bearing bone. I trusted this doctor because he saved my finger. Please note at this point in my life, I would have been devastated to have to go through life without a finger. A few days later, after the operation on my leg, the doctor told me that I was injured during surgery but it would heal.

After three years, 15 operations, and over 350 hospital days, I had to have my leg amputated. Through litigation, I found out that the x-rays used in the operating room showed a completely healed leg (a healed broken bone will cause pain some-times for years). The doctor neglected to irrigate properly during surgery. He burned through the bone and soft tissue leaving an opening in the flesh.

The bone died and the opening in the flesh became a source for numerous skin and bone infections. I lost my leg as a result of an injury that happened during unnecessary surgery.

The miraculous part of all of this is that I fully trusted God in all of it. I woke up from surgery knowing that God was going to use me as an amputee. I felt His arms embracing me and carrying me through that transition to the journey I am on today. Three years earlier, I could not deal with losing a finger and now, with my strength through Jesus, I was accepting the loss of a leg.

Six months after my leg was amputated, I took a trip out west with another amputee. He was going to walk across the United States to encourage other amputees. On our way we stopped in Little Rock, Arkansas and attended an AA meeting. There was a woman at the meeting whose 18 month old grandson was going to lose his leg. She was a wreck thinking he would live a dismal life and would be considered a freak. When she saw how well my friend and I were doing she said it gave her faith that her grandson would live a productive life, and knowing this, she felt strong enough to endure his surgery. I thanked Jesus for using me to bring hope to this dear grandmother.

My friend did not go through with the walk across the U.S. He could not raise what he felt was enough financial support. I wanted to do it all on faith that God would provide the means, but he did not feel the same way.

We came home and, within a few months, I met a woman and got involved in a three year relationship. She was a schoolteacher and I spoke to her sixth and eighth grade students about "differently-abled" people. I walked into the class with my prosthesis covered by long pants. I walk very well so the students could not tell that I was an amputee. After I built a rapport with them, I asked the class to try to identify my disability. They could not. Then I left the room and came back without my prosthesis, on crutches. I asked the students if they would have treated me any differently had I looked like that when they first met me. Most of them said yes, they would have seen me differently and would not have felt as comfortable talking with me. When asked why, they admitted their prejudices. I asked them why they did not treat me with the same prejudices. They said it was because they got to know me first as a person just like anyone else. They got the point!

I thank Jesus for using me to touch these children's lives. I trust that this will prevent some cruelty that kids often impose on those who are different. I believe that these young lives were touched in a positive way and that some of these young people will pass on what they learned. "We know that all things work together for good for those who love God, who are the called according to His purpose." Even amputations!

About six years ago, I started attending a gay affirming church. It felt good to worship God with people who love and respect me just as I am. A few years after I started attending this church, I went to a weekend Christian conference with the pastor and some other people from church. God touched me tremendously that weekend. He reminded me of the call to the ministry when I was 12 years old. He also reminded me about that walk across the U.S. I had a great desire to do God's will. I began praying, fasting, meditating, and studying God's Word more than ever.

I knew I had to get out of the relationship that I was in. My partner was not a Christian and the life we lived together was a life of strife and materialism. I had received a settlement for my leg injury and I was throwing the money away on a big house, expensive cars, and travel. She was from a wealthy family and I tried to keep up with her expensive tastes. I chose this woman over God and I was not attending church regularly. She became involved in some illegal activity and the relationship ended with her in jail.

I spent several days fasting, praying and seeking God's will. Within a year, I was out of the big house and got rid of the expensive cars (not that these things are bad, but they were bad for me because I became too materialistic and less spiritual). I began attending church on a regular basis. God brought another woman into my life, a good Christian woman who was the pastor of another church in the same city. We both knew that God brought us together and we had a Holy Union six months later.

We have been together five years now. We have been ministering together since the day God brought us together. I was ordained and have joined the church where my partner is the pastor. I have been installed as the pastor of evangelism. I will be graduating Bible college next month and will begin graduate studies.

I never did discover what makes little girls hurt so much. But I did discover who carries little girls through the pain and how He strengthens us to be special messengers for Him. God is still doing great and mighty things in my life. Who knows, I may walk across the U.S. someday, and, if I do, I will be spreading the love of Jesus from the beaches of San Diego to the Jersey shores.

___ Carrie Crosse

Freedom Behind Bars

Like many people, I was raised in a broken home. My parents divorced when I was seven and my mom took me, my brother, who was a year younger, and my two year old sister with her. She did her best to raise us right and often worked two jobs. Until I was 12, she took us to church regularly, first to a Baptist church and then to a Seventh Day Adventist church. We moved frequently, then settled for a few years in rural Northeast Pennsylvania. When I turned 13, we moved to New York City. Initially, I didn't fit in; those "city" kids were alien to me. Then, when I did, it was with the wrong crowd.

I stayed in trouble with the law and was charged with robbery when I was 14 years old. This was New York in the 70's, and all I got was more and more probation. I tried to stay with my dad a few times, but that never lasted more than a month.

When I turned 15, I went to stay with my aunt and uncle. This was heaven to me! I had both "parents," a nice home, and we attended a Bible teaching Protestant church. They enrolled me in a Protestant private school. For a year I did really well and enjoyed it immensely. I thought I finally found my life.

However, when I turned 16, I became very rebellious. One day I got into an argument with a family friend. He threw it in my face that my aunt and uncle felt I was a burden and didn't want me. The truth was that my aunt and uncle had gone to him for advice, since he had teenage children of his own. He twisted what was actually said during those conversations, which fed my rebellion. I left them. I stayed with numerous friends and family, then hitch-hiked to Florida. I rented a trailer and tried to make a go of it. But I was very wild. I partied too much and lost it all. Not knowing what to do, I went to Iowa to stay with my dad, but again, a month later it was out the door for me. I went back to Pennsylvania and bummed around.

At 17 I decided to join the Army. I took the test and passed, and was waiting for the physical date. During that wait, I went to a party and met a dude who wanted to do some robberies. I went with him. We came back, got my brother, and traveled the east coast, robbing and partying. It came to an end in New Hampshire, where we were all arrested.

Danny and I both got 1-10 years in prison. My 16 year old brother was sent to a juvenile center. Since I was 17, I went to Concord State Prison. Luckily, I was a decent size at 6 foot, 180 pounds. I had some fights but nothing serious. I only did a year and got out. My brother was released right behind me. We lived with my mom again, just until I could get on my feet. Though I did try at first, I could only get a job making $90 a week. I was still too wild and now I had a chip on my shoulder.

After a few months, I had my fill. I was at a party when we ran out of liquor. There were six of us. We all piled into a car and went to a gas station. Three of us got out and robbed it. We then headed down the east coast, pulling robberies and partying. This came to an end in Santa Rosa County, Florida. They arrested all six of us on robbery. My brother, a friend, and I made pleas to cut the others free. Danny got 10 years, my brother 15, and I

173

got 30 years. We all went to the same prison. A few months later, I was notified of a different robbery charge. I was taken back to court. They offered me 10 years if I would roll on my partners. I refused, went to trial, was found guilty and got life in prison. I was sent to a different prison.

I began reading the Bible and went to church, but wasn't that serious about it. Then I met an "Odinist." I'd never heard of that before. It is a pagan religion that believes in the old Nordic gods. I put down the Bible and got heavily into this cult. I also got into the dope and loaning business. A few years passed and I was deeper into it all. I was backing a friend in a confrontation and stabbed a dude. I got transferred, but fell right back into the same type of crowd. We had our religious Odinist services and propagated our beliefs. After a couple years there, I was locked up and then transferred, after being instrumental in an escape plot.

I ended up at UCI, the old rock. There I met a man who was a satanic high priest, who was not like the new age fads such as Anton Levy, but the old masters such as Allistar Crowley, Eliphas Levi, and McGregor. I threw myself into this, heart and soul, and devoted a lot of time and energy into the study and practice. I filed petitions to receive study material and to continue practicing. It took years, but we won and were able to get a lot for study use and to make any tools we needed for rituals.

At the same time, I also began getting involved with a prison gang called the "Unforgiven" and was deeper into dope, gambling, and other prison vices. I always had at least one "boy," the term for a "bottom" in prison. Some I cared for, but most I just looked on as property for my enjoyment. I would go to war over them, just like any other property of mine.

After a few years, I believed things were going as well as can be for one locked up in prison. Money, drugs, and "butt"; I had plenty, so I was happy and felt they were all blessings from my god Lucifer. Then, one day while I was high on drugs, an officer found my dope stash and went to take it. I took it from him and ate it. It was too much and I O.D.'d. They restarted my heart three times. I recovered. At the hospital I asked to use the bathroom, and then tried to go through the ceiling to escape, but was caught. Back at prison I was put on close management, which is prolonged confinement. After nine months, me and a dude got into a fight with six others. One guy got his throat cut. They sent me to another prison, where a mix up in paperwork got me put into the regular population.

I started right back in business, got me a fine boy, and went back to my religious practices with Lucifer. After only a month, I was involved in some racial disturbances, which once again landed me in close management. I was there for 11 months. I used this time to build up my library and increased my studies. Once back in the general population, I again involved myself in another disturbance after only two weeks.

This time I was sent to another prison, and after a year, they sent me to another prison. There I met a bunch of old cronies and was back in business. I also continued to propagate my satanic doctrine, especially on the new, younger inmates. I showed them how much fun Satan was with drugs, wild sex, and all that one can have in prison.

I used to go around with sacks of dope and "buy souls," especially around the chapel. I'd go there to get the Christians high and lure them away from the chapel. I'd give them books and literature and show them that they could "belong" and be "one of us," which so many wanted for security and well being.

A couple of years later, and two more prisons, I was involved in the same practices with new inmates. I got six more years added to my life sentence after stabbing a dude who crossed me. I was sent to the prison in Starke, Florida.

This was the bottom of the line. I was put on close management again, but I had quite a library and spent all my time studying. I met up with the dude who first got me into Satanism and a couple more who were seriously into it for many years. I was taken to even greater depths. I got into more trouble once again and was put under investigation. Somehow this was a turning point. I found myself hanging around a couple of the same Christians I used to make fun of. Miraculously, for some reason I began to listen to them.

Soon after officers confiscated 33 books of mine on the occult. They said I was a leader of a Satan group, and was planning escapes. Not true, but now I had nothing to read. When my brother heard of my plight, he sent me a study Bible, as did an old couple who had been trying for years to bring me to Christ. After talking to my new friends and receiving these Bibles, I began to read them.

A conviction came over me, and although I fought it, I eventually could no longer. I poured it all out to God and felt peace come over me. I accepted His Son Jesus as my Savior, Lord and King. There is no way to put into words how amazing it felt or explain the way my life has so dramatically turned around. I can testify that the power of God in my heart has enabled me to change. It is like night and day. I have gone from extreme darkness into light. I am no longer involved in the evil that I was so intimate with for years. Christ has given me a new heart. I am so blessed to have finally been "saved" from myself and the evil forces at work all around me. I cannot change my past, but I know that God has forgiven me, wiped me clean, and given me a new life.

Physically I am still in bondage, but my spirit has been set free in Christ. After they were returned to me, I destroyed the 33 occult books, as I no longer had use for them. I do have some fellowship in prison, as God has sent me a reverend and two Christian friends who have been of great help and comfort to me. I have a great desire to learn the truths of God and study the Bible as much as I can. I even communicate with a few believers on the outside by mail, who have helped instruct me in my studies and Christian growth.

It has not been an easy path, to say the least. My old cronies feel as if I'm a traitor, but my life is God's. I'm not perfect, but I study His Word diligently and desire to be a vessel for His use. I pray that all those I used and abused can forgive me. I now share the love God has put in my heart, as only He can do. Though I've spent the last 20 years in prison doing Satan's work, I pray that I can spend even more time doing God's work.

It's Always Something

I was born to a very poor family in 1941. My father died when I was seven and left mother with three small children to raise. She was 40 but mentally unstable. I was verbally, physically, emotionally and sexually abused all my life: sexually, by my mother, two brothers, and husband. After several years of marriage and four children, I got divorced. My husband took the children in the divorce. My older sister later adopted all of them. All this and I was only 24.

After my divorce, I came out of the closet. My mother was a very strict, religious fanatic and raised us in a fundamental religion. I did know about God and even accepted Jesus when I was seven. The messages were confusing though, and I didn't know the true loving God until much later.

After I lost my children in the divorce, I turned my back on Christ. I believed a good God could never have allowed all the terrible things that had happened to me, one of His children. This led me into utter despair. I drank, did drugs, frequented bars and clubs, had bad relationships and one night stands, and tried very hard to get myself killed. I did this for seven solid years.

I finally met a woman and fell in love. She didn't drink or do drugs, so I quit the drugs and cut back on the drinking. I started to think more clearly and started missing God in my life. My oldest daughter then got pregnant and came to live with us. After baby B.J. was born, she felt she couldn't handle him and gave me custody of him. I thought maybe God was giving me another chance to be a mother. I knew B.J. needed to learn about Jesus and I started to believe again.

B.J. was killed in a car accident when he was only five. I got really angry at God, cursed Him, and turned away from Him once again. I swore I could not love a God that allowed me to lose my children twice. I got mad if anyone even mentioned God to me. I turned 40 that year.

Two years later I was in a good relationship and was doing well in my own business. But I knew something wasn't right, something was missing. I decided to turn my life back over to God. My life without Christ was filled with bad decisions, poor judgment and bad consequences. I had no peace. I knew true peace would only come through faith and trust in Him.

Having faith in God doesn't mean nothing bad will happen to you. I know from first hand. As soon as I turned back to Him, things went crazy. My partner left me and my business began to fail. I went into a deep depression. I found myself in another abusive relationship and thought I was losing my mind. I was. Did I really turn back to God, completely trusting in Him to guide me? Or was this simply what I had to go through to test and strengthen my faith?

Persistent faith, along with antidepressants, helped me regain myself. But still, I was to endure more. My partner left me with a load of bills, and had run my credit cards to the max. I was working but had to file for bankruptcy. With my sister's help, I was beginning to get back on my feet, but I developed severe arthritis and lost my job. I started college and took odd jobs. It took four years to be granted Social Security Disability. Through it all, God took care of me. I never went hungry or became homeless. I trusted in Him, even though my situation seemed to keep getting worse, because I knew He would do what was best for me in the long run. Even when my faith waned, He never abandoned me.

Looking back at all my pain and suffering, I see God holding my hand, keeping me alive, allowing me to endure all I did to grow in faith, maturity and love. I will certainly understand and appreciate the glories of heaven. He protected me from myself, for if it were not for His love and grace, I would have taken my own life. But that is not what He had planned for me. He even got me through a year stay at a tuberculosis hospital, when no one thought I would recover. I am now at peace with God, myself and the world. He has blessed me with a life-time partnership with a wonderful woman. I have strength and courage because of Him. He affords me wonderful opportunities to testify to His unconditional love for all. I couldn't have expected a greater reward.

Remember my brother who abused me? He came to me for care when he was suffering with cancer. Before he died, he asked me twice to forgive him. I answered, "Jesus died for you, God forgives you, and so do I."

Does the End Justify the Means?

I am the office manager for two doctors. Some of my responsibilities include: signing in patients, scheduling appointments, answering the phone, billing and insurance. I've been very happy with this job. As an openly gay man, the doctors I work for have treated me exceptionally well. I have always taken my work seriously and consider myself reliable and professional. The patients are my first concern, and I always try to remember that they are there because they don't feel well.

The former office manager left due to poor health. Although no one was happy about her illness, the doctors and staff were glad that she left. She was always trying to preach to the patients and staff about her religious beliefs. It was becoming uncomfortable for everyone. During my interview I was told of this past situation, and was advised by the doctors not to discuss or argue religious or political issues in the work place. With that in mind, I began my new job.

I have been in the office for over a year and I've gotten to know the patients. There is one woman who frequently talks about her church. I had heard of this church from other patients. The pastor speaks on Christian radio. He and the church are well known.

One morning recently, this same woman came in for her appointment. While waiting to see the doctor, she invited me to her church. I already knew that church's policy on gay people. But since she was inviting me, I wanted to give her the opportunity to be honest with me. So, I responded, "Sure, as long as I can bring my partner." She said that if we came to her church we would both surely see the error of our ways and would be changed. Then she told me that her pastor had recently counseled with a prostitute in his office, so why wouldn't he allow two gay men to visit the church? There were other people in the waiting room. At point I was embarrassed, for her and myself. To expedite things, I came right out and asked her how her minister *really* felt regarding gay people. Instead of being forthright, she danced around the question, and did not tell me the truth.

At that point, I excused myself to go to the bathroom. She followed me into the bathroom repeating over and over that I needed to see the error of my ways! I was shocked at her behavior and completely uncomfortable with the situation. Finally, I told her I already knew how her minister felt from other patients. She became very emotional and started to cry. At this point, I was getting very concerned about my job. I politely, but firmly, told her I could no longer engage in this conversation, that it was inappropriate for my workplace, or any other place for that matter.

I believe her tears were the result of feeling let down by the others from her church that had already told me how the church really felt about homosexuals. She wanted me to have an opportunity to attend the church and be changed. I cannot imagine that deception is the ideal way to invite people to church. I have heard of similar situations happening to other gay people, but this was a first for me.

Finally, the nurse summoned her and led her to one of the examining rooms. The woman then proceeded to explain to the nurse how I needed to see the error of my ways. The nurse (not gay) stood up for me and told the woman that this was not the time or place to discuss such things.

I was raised by two loving parents who knew that I was different at an early age. My dad was an avid outdoors man and taught me to hunt and fish. I went everywhere with him. When I became an adult, I was honest with my parents. Both of them accepted me and continue to love me. I have been in a monogamous relationship with my partner for over three years. I do not flaunt my homosexuality, but I am honest about it. I don't look for trouble. I try to be friendly and courteous to everyone.

At night, when I lay my head on my pillow, I say my prayers and sense God's presence with me. I believe and accept that Jesus is the Son of God. I am very thankful that I have such peace with God.

I realize that it is difficult for many people to understand homosexuality, including homosexuals themselves, but sometimes there are no pat answers regarding some things in life. I would like to attend a church, but if I am not welcomed by a group of people, I know that God welcomes me and is with me no matter where I am. My parents, sisters, and partner love me. I am greatly blessed.

Light From the
Pages of Tolstoy

Many a Jew, when asked what his religious creed is, will think it sufficient to say, "I do not believe in Jesus." In the third chapter of the book of Romans, the Apostle Paul poses these questions: "Then what advantage has the Jew? Or what is the value of circumcision?" He answers his own question by reminding the Roman Christians of the Jews' privilege in having been entrusted with the Word of God. Had the great apostle lived in later times, he might have added another advantage the Jew enjoys: he does not grow up sitting on a church pew assuming that he is a Christian.

My family certainly identified with Jewish culture, but religious observance was confined to weekly synagogue attendance and the celebration of a few holidays. You wouldn't find sausage with

milk gravy or pork barbecue in our house, but neither would you find strict adherence to the tenets of
kosher housekeeping and cooking.

I had a certain predilection for the few
snatches of the Old Testament to which I was
exposed as a child. I remember being deeply
impressed by the fact that the God of Israel had
ignored the venerable priest Eli and had chosen
instead to speak to Samuel, then a little boy. As soon
as I was taught the ten commandments, I wanted
to keep every one of them perfectly. At one point I
even announced to my parents my intention of
becoming a rabbi.

Years before I was born, my aunt Yvette
converted to Christian Science. Occasionally she
would take me with her to church, my parents
having no objection. I was, at the time, too young
to understand the readings, but I enjoyed singing
the hymns. In awe I remember listening to "Come
let us adore Him, Christ the Lord," but I didn't
understand it.

In my mid-teens I stopped attending
synagogue, and my parents made no great issue of
the lapse. They encouraged me in my academic and

musical pursuits, and in anything else they thought would enable me to prosper.

By the time I was in college, I was a self-proclaimed agnostic. It was not that I had consciously rejected God; I simply entertained no hope that He could ever be satisfactorily known. I realized, mostly from reading, that there were--or at least once had been--people who claimed to believe in God and in Jesus Christ. I was secretly envious of them. Between them and me I saw two great barriers: my Jewishness and my unbelief. I didn't know how such people got their faith, but I assumed that it had something to do with having been brought up in a Lutheran, Methodist, or Baptist home. Yet oddly enough, I never quite lost a wistfulness for Jesus Christ.

At college in New York, even those feeble religious gropings were forgotten as I threw myself headlong into what the city offered to young hedonists in the 1960's. I sinned recklessly, committing acts and speaking words which even today cause me painful remorse. I had discarded my parents' "value system" of personal comfort and convenience, but I had none of my own with which to replace it.

Eventually, I graduated from NYU, completed a one year graduate study at Columbia University, and accepted my first professional job at the library of the City College of New York. I tackled my new responsibilities with the excessive zeal which has characterized every stage of my life before and since. I enjoyed the privilege of faculty status, the bright professional prospects, and, of course, the pleasures that a real salary could purchase. But inwardly I was a desperately unhappy person.

Relations with my parents were both intermittent and stormy. I had seduced and abandoned a childhood sweetheart. I very much wanted love and stability, but I was deeply afraid of commitment in any form. I was living as the Apostle Paul wrote to Titus, "foolish, disobedient, led astray, slaves to various passions and pleasures, passing our days in malice and envy, despicable, hating one another." As do many people, I began to blame my environment for my problems; I had to get out of New York!

The opportunity came sooner than I expected. On vacation in northern Europe, in the summer of 1970, I had fallen in love with

Copenhagen, Denmark. "This is it," I thought, "the quiet, the Old World culture, the gracious Danish people; I will move to Denmark!" Having met someone who offered me space in his flat, I flew back to New York, took a Berlitz course in Danish, quit my job, and flew back to Copenhagen in September.

Looking back, it is hard to know whether my courage or my stupidity is more to be marveled at. Of course, with my rudimentary grasp of the language, there was little work available to me in Copenhagen, and certainly nothing of a professional nature. I was close to panic. I could have returned directly to New York, but I was too ashamed to admit my folly. I decided that as long as I was on the east side of the Atlantic, I would make an effort to find work where I could at least speak the language. After identifying some job openings in London, I flew there in November.

In London, I went on a few interviews. In between, there were long stretches of depressing inactivity and rich opportunities for self-flagellation. I had recently picked up a paperback copy of Leo Tolstoy's novel, *Anna Karenina.* It did for me exactly what I wanted a piece of literature to do at that time; it made me forget my own sorrows in order to identify with those of someone else.

Where should an unemployed librarian more naturally gravitate to then an open library? With plenty of time on my hands, I became a regular visitor to the humanities reading room of the University of London. On the mezzanine, my eye was caught one day by a handsome bound set: the complete works of Count Lev Nikolayevich Tolstoy, in English translation. Having fresh memories of my recent reading of *Anna Karenina,* I decided to sample more of this author. I was intrigued by the title of another Tolstoy book I pulled off the shelf: *What I Believe.* I remember thinking, "That is an odd title for a novel." Opening to the introduction, I read the following statements:

"I lived in the world for fifty-five years, and after the first fourteen or fifteen of childhood I was for thirty-five years a nihilist in the real meaning of that word, that is to say, not a Socialist or revolutionary, as those words are generally understood, but a nihilist in the sense of an absence of any belief. Five years ago I came to believe in Christ's teaching, and my life suddenly changed; I ceased to desire what I had previously desired, and began to desire what I formerly did not want."

Tolstoy's words riveted me. I turned page after page, as one of the world's greatest authors described his spiritual odyssey in simple but compelling words. After a while, I went downstairs and took a place at one of the reading tables. I became aware of a voice speaking as if it were from inside my own soul, (which I would have denied possessing), saying, "This is it; this is what you have been looking for." At the same time, I realized that the reading room, rather poorly illuminated on a gray London afternoon, had become brilliantly lit. Scarcely pausing to notice, I went back to my reading.

From 9:00 a.m. until closing time at 5:00 p.m. I continued reading. What I now recognize as a partial and imperfect view of Christianity, was for me then a blinding flash of revelation in the gross darkness of my ignorance and confusion. I knew that I never again could live as I had before, now that the majesty of Christ's teaching had been laid before me.

A few days later I returned to New York. I had no job, no apartment and no prospects for either, but it didn't matter to me anymore. A couple of friends let me stay in a spare room about six by eight feet: I was thrilled to have it. I bought a King James Bible, and not knowing any better, I began to read it straight through from Genesis onward. I read other things too. I remember leafing through Jung, *The Varieties of Religious Experience* by William James, and of course, *The Village Voice*. In the latter I came across a classified ad stating, "We are Jews who love Jesus. Come see us." Noting the address, I did just that. To my surprise, the chapel of the American Board of Missions to the Jews (now Chosen People Ministries) was located on West 72nd Street, on the very route I had taken weekly on my way to group therapy sessions for two years.

At the mission, I came under the teaching and preaching of several ministers, including Art Katz, a well known evangelist and author. Katz took a particular interest in me, and invited me to attend a prayer meeting with a Japanese brother. As Katz and his friend sought the Lord with groans and tears, I watched with big saucer eyes. One Sunday, in response to one of Katz's sermons in the chapel, I went forward to receive my Messiah. A little while later I was baptized there.

There was still the small matter of employment. City College of New York did not want me back, and I wasn't sure I wanted to remain in the city anyway. I took a job at the State University at Potsdam, New York, not far from the Canadian border, in March 1971.

I didn't know much about being a Christian, but I thought that attending a church had something to do with it. There was a small group of believers in Potsdam which was dissatisfied with the mainstream churches in the area, and had formed its own interdenominational church, which the pastor dubbed "Koinonia," the Greek term for "fellowship." The charismatic movement had by this time spread across the country from the west coast to New York. To my dismay, that same scary "Holy Spirit" which had so spooked me in New York City was there in Potsdam too! Almost every week I was hearing about someone else "being filled" and talking in "new tongues."

Meanwhile, I was trying to figure out just exactly what it was that I believed. I thought that affiliating with the right denomination was very important, but which one was the right one? I looked into the Jehovah's Witnesses, the Swedenborgians, the Mennonites, the Hutterites, and the Adventists, among others. I was reading the Bible at this time and praying as well, but more dutifully than joyfully. I was approaching faith as an intellectual problem to be solved, not as a life to be lived in the strength and wisdom given by God.

Among my friends was a couple just a few years older than I, but many years more mature in the Lord. their ministry to me was mostly to show friendship and to listen patiently to my latest religious theories. One day Jack and Vi invited me over to listen to a tape of the testimony of a Presbyterian minister. I found myself drawn in by his words, as he described how, after years of a fruitless ministry, he had come into a new place of power with God and men. In that quiet room, alongside my longsuffering friends, I felt my heart crying out for the spiritual reality which this minister was describing: "On that day all the springs of the great deep burst forth," as I no longer resisted God's desire to baptize me with his Holy Spirit. What I experienced, as my friends prayed for me, is what Charles Finney described 150 years earlier:

"The Holy Ghost seemed to go through me, body and soul. I could feel the impression, like a wave of electricity, going through and through me. Indeed it seemed to come in waves and waves of liquid love, for I could not express it any other way. It seemed like the very breath of God."

We must now fast forward more than 20 years: past a 13 year marriage, two children, many geographical moves, a ruined career, another risen from its ashes, four years of missionary work, and lots of detours, dead ends, and perplexities of sundry kinds.

More than thirty years have passed between the day I was baptized and the events of September 11, 2001. I wonder what lies before the American church? Unlike the Apostle John, I have had no visions of the future. This I know: the faithful God, the covenant keeping God, the God of Abraham, of Isaac, and Jacob, will not disappoint His children who look to Him in expectant faith, seeking His blessing on their churches, their families, and their nation. The clouds above are dark and ominous. Will they flash with the lightening of God's righteous judgement, or will they pour out the abundant rains of life-giving revival? The choice is as much in our hands as in God's:

"If my people who are called by my name humble themselves, pray, seek my face, and turn from their wicked ways, then I will hear from heaven, and will forgive their sin and heal their land" (2 Chronicles 7:14)

___ a Hebrew Christian

In 1993 Aaron became very involved with a local church in Charlotte, North Carolina. He was invited to give a course on prayer and seized the opportunity. For several months he read everything he could find in the Scriptures and from experienced Christians on the subject. After the course, he developed a hunger to meet with other Christians who recognized the importance and power of prayer. He attended weekly evening prayer meetings, led a midweek prayer class and participated in a Saturday morning men's prayer group. Aaron reports these years among the happiest and most joyful of his life.

In September, 1998, this all came to an abrupt end when a visitor to the church reported to the administration that Aaron was gay. Within 24 hours, three elders, two of them his close friends, were at his house asking for his set of the church keys, and requesting that he never return to the church.

For the next year and a half Aaron was in a painful, broken state, yet his faith never wavered and he continued in prayer. Rejected by the organized church, he knew that God still loved him and accepted him as he was: a Hebrew Christian who was gay.

Aaron still wanted to serve the Lord, but did not look to join another church group or denomination. He believed that his peace and joy was based upon his personal relationship with the Lord, and not on belonging to a specific church. God answered his prayers and directed him to people who he would not have ordinarily sought out. He felt led to reach out to specific groups of Cambodians and Chinese-Americans. Through their own mainline churches, Aaron has been ministering independently to these people. He teaches Sunday school to Cambodian youth, and tutors Christian Chinese Americans in English. Aaron has also joyfully witnessed his partner, a lifetime churchgoer, accept Jesus into his life. They have been together for 13 years.

You've Got Mail

The following questions and answers are an excerpt from an e-mail dialogue I had with a stranger, a woman who is a heterosexual Christian. She was curious about gay people who claim to be Christian, who accept and have faith in Jesus Christ. As a gay person and a believer in Christ, I did my best to answer her questions honestly.

Subject: Re: Questions
Date: Sat, 27 Jun 01:04:33
From: Mary Phil4.13@angel.com
To: Traci@blueskies.com

Traci: I hope this e-mail finds you well. I'm curious; I am a Christian woman (not lesbian) and have seen on some websites ministers who are gay. I have a few questions. How can one be a minister and gay at the same time? In fact, how can a gay person be a Christian at all?

Mary: Your question implies that homosexuality in and of itself is sinful. I will address that in other areas of this e-mail.

Some gay people are ministers of the gospel for the same reason some heterosexual people are ministers; they believe they've been "called of God." Some people in the institutional churches spend an exorbitant amount of time condemning homosexuality, although Jesus himself never once mentioned it. God has called on another group of people to go to homosexuals with the gospel of peace (Ephesians 6:15) and reconciliation (Romans 5:10; 2 Corinthians 5:18,19,20; Colossians 1:20,21; Ephesians 2;16). Believers who are gay themselves are ministering to the gay community. Gay people all over the country are finding faith in Christ. God accepts "...everyone who believes in Him..." (John 3:16).

A more appropriate question is: how does *anyone* come to find peace and joy in His salvation? The answer is in Paul's letter to the Romans; "If you confess with your lips that Jesus is Lord and believe in your heart that God raised him from the dead, you will be saved...the same Lord is Lord of *all* and is generous to *all* who call on him, for, *everyone* who calls on the name of the Lord shall be saved" (Romans 10:9,12,13). Many gay people are doing this very thing.

Traci: But doesn't the church (Catholic and Protestant) say homosexuality is wrong and sinful?
Mary: Only God is infallible, not the institutional church, which is made up of men. Many people still believe that whatever "the church" says is the truth. Meanwhile, there have been times in history when the institutional church failed to function in the spirit of Christ. The reason there are so many factions in some denominations is because of theological differences regarding Bible interpretation. There were many splits in the churches in this country over the issue of slavery, back in the 1800's. Something similar is happening now regarding the issue of homosexuality. There are groups of Baptists, Methodists, Presbyterians, Lutherans, and others, who are in disagreement over whether or not homosexuality is sinful, who are breaking away from their denominational lines. So, not all churches and Christians are opposed to gay people.

At one time in history the Church had great political power and used Scripture to wield its control over the masses. The leadership of the Church interpreted the Bible and inferred that the common man could not understand Scripture for himself. The Bible was not available to everyone. Today we have no excuse; we have Bibles, concordances, and a great deal of reference material to help us study. The Apostle Paul told Timothy to study the word of God (the Scriptures), (2 Timothy 2:15).During the lifetime of Paul and Timothy there was no institutional church. People met in homes and were guided by the Holy Spirit. The institutional church exists now, but that does not remove the responsibility from individuals to study for themselves and come to prayerful conclusions, not only about homosexuality, but also all theological questions and controversies regarding traditionally accepted interpretations and doctrines.

Unfortunately, we are at a great impasse over interpretation of Scripture in relation to this subject. We are at a stalemate. The main question is whether or not a homosexual is born that way or not. If it could be proven that homosexuality is inborn (genetics, DNA), then the institutional church might be appeased. Since this has not yet been proven, we remain in this uncomfortable stalemate and the institutional church relentlessly continues to single out and condemn homosexuality. Homosexuals who believe they are inherently different, yet have no proof, find no peace or comfort offered to them by the church. When the church becomes the "oppressor," instead of reaching out with the light and grace of God to *all* people, then it is no longer a place of solace and unconditional love. The efficacy of the institutional churches as "beacons of divine light" are in question by many. Some wonder if the church has lost its focus and sense of mission.

Traci: Why do you call it the "institutional church"?

Mary: There is a significant difference between the organized churches ("institutional") and the "body of Christ." The body of Christ is the true spiritual church of the Bible. True believers in Christ are members of *that* spiritual body (1 Corinthians 12:12; 12:27; and Colossians 1:18). Some people are under the impression that every church-goer and church leader is a Christian. Not so. Only those who truly believe and have accepted Christ as their Saviour are truly Christians and members of the true body of Christ.

Traci: But doesn't the Bible say that homosexuality is wrong? The word homosexual is in my New King James Version.

Mary: The word "homosexual" does not appear in the original Greek in the New Testament, or in the original King James version and other older versions, since this word was not actually coined until the 1800's, long after the Bible itself and older translations were written.

There are many new Bible versions that have incorrectly translated several Greek words as "homosexual." This biased and unscholarly approach to translation has confused many people. These translations conveniently support the wave of condemnation coming from the churches. Use a concordance and view the Hebrew and Greek words for yourself.

I think about the people that Luke wrote about in Acts, the Bereans. They searched the Scriptures daily to see if the things they heard were true (Acts 17:10-11). Don't just believe everything you hear. When the Scriptures traditionally used to condemn homosexuality are studied in their proper translation and context, it

208

becomes evident that they are not referring to loving, monogamous, same-sex relationships, but acts such as male prostitution, pedophilia, violence, domination, and idol worship. There are many excellent books available on this subject. I also highly recommend doing a word study using a concordance of the Bible, which is an excellent way to study the original Hebrew and Greek words. The newer versions of the Bible support the mainline, evangelical doctrine regarding this issue, but if you check the Greek and Hebrew it is another story. Many people are lazy and just believe what they hear and will not study. I have heard many well known preachers and Bible teachers complain that the average Christian is Bible illiterate. I agree with them. This leads to multitudes becoming "sheep," who follow their leaders without question. This is extremely dangerous.

Traci: Wouldn't it be better if homosexuals just stayed celibate?

Mary: The Apostle Paul wrote to the unmarried and widows and told them that it was better to live like him (unmarried) so they could focus all their attention on serving the Lord (1 Corinthians 7:8-9). But in reality, how many heterosexual Christians make that kind of commitment, yet expect homosexuals to uphold that commitment?

When a man believes he has been called to the priesthood, he makes a voluntary vow to stay celibate. I've always thought that was a remarkable endeavor, and have wondered how many were actually able to uphold such a strict requirement of the Church (not the Bible). Is it really feasible that the everyday homosexual involuntarily make a vow to never engage in sexual intimacy?

Does a priest, "a man of God," ever struggle with basic human desires? If this is true for a priest, how much more are we asking of the "average homosexual"? Does the Bible say to involuntarily repress these desires completely? Could you live like that?

What do you actually mean by "celibate"? Does it mean no intimacy with anyone ever in your whole entire life? No companion, no holding hands, no hugs? In other words, a homosexual is not permitted to express any feelings at all? Are they permitted to have any relationship which is loving and intimate? Did God create these people for a life of loneliness? I personally don't believe that God operates like that.

Traci: We are not supposed to do what pleases our flesh, but only what pleases God. We must not practice homosexuality (sexual immorality, murder, adultery, etc.).

Mary: There are people who call themselves Christians, who consider homosexuals equal to murderers. Homosexuality is automatically assumed to be sexual immorality. Many heterosexuals practice deviant, immoral, sexual behavior: pornography, pedophilia, promiscuity, and cheating on spouses (adultery), to mention a few. If homosexuals engage in similar behavior they are also sinning. So, homosexuals can be immoral, but not simply because they are homosexual.

I am a believer in Christ and gay. I can tell you that I greatly mistrust the organized church and its followers. I wonder if mainline, straight Christians realize how frightening they appear at times. It is so sad, yet I consider many of them brothers and sisters in Christ, even though I've been ostracized from the *family*. It is no wonder the gay community is so frustrated and angry. Where is the gospel of the peace of God? How in the world is the gospel of the peace of God going to be proclaimed to them by Christians, when the very ones claiming to possess the gospel are accusing gay people of being guilty of things equal to murder? If the gay people are "lost," many Christians are doing a great job of driving them further and further away from the gospel. I wonder what God thinks about this!

Also, being gay is not about "pleasing the flesh" any more than a heterosexual is "pleasing the flesh" by having a wife, husband, girlfriend or boyfriend. Are these relationships only about sex? Do those people only think about sex continuously? Neither do gay people! I always get the feeling that Christian heterosexuals think that homosexuals are all wild and uncontrollable, and have sex continuously. There are promiscuous, perverted homosexuals just as there are promiscuous, perverted heterosexuals. There is no one without sin (Romans 3:23).

Traci: Aren't "family values" being violated by homosexuals?
Mary: Exactly what do you mean by the clichè, "family values"? Values can change from family to family, culture to culture, and there are differences even within the institutional churches. The Apostle Paul said that we should "...hold fast the form of sound words..." (2 Timothy 1:13, KJV). I take that to mean scriptural terminology, not phrases and slogans coined by churches. Clichès can become mantras, which can be overused and revered above Scripture itself. That is the danger of using words and slogans which are not "sound."

In 1861 the Civil War began. One of the hot issues was the right to own slaves. It was a moral issue.

Many Christians owned slaves. Churches split and families fought and killed each other over it. Were those good family values?

This clichè is not necessarily in sync with God's values, and His unconditional love. Here is my question: if one is loving, compassionate, has faith in Jesus, and yet is homosexual, how does that interfere with your family's values? Homosexuals are not trying to dissolve families. In fact, most want a stable, loving family of their own.

Traci: I guess you're right about that, but I still don't understand how you can continue to be gay. Wouldn't it just be easier to change?

Mary: Let me ask you a couple of questions: are you right-handed or left-handed? Is your handedness a "choice"? What if you were required to change your predominant hand? Would that be possible for you? Did you know that at one time in history being left-handed was considered sinister by the organized church, which influenced the rest of society? Do you think that being left-handed in those days was a choice? I wonder if the church has ever apologized to those poor left-handers. I also wonder how those left-handed people fared psychologically and emotionally. Did they feel different? You better believe it. Did they ever get angry? How many left-handers were "in the closet" to lessen the pain of being labeled evil? Most of all, I wonder if the dictates of the organized church of the time found favor in the eyes of God? So, wouldn't it be easier to be right-handed even though you may be left-handed? After all, most of the world is right-handed. Yes, it would be easier in some ways, but is it natural? Would you be able to live a productive life? Something to think about.

We continue being gay because that is our true nature. We are different *only* in that we are gay. We work, pay bills, go shopping, go to school, and are concerned about the world. Many people laughingly stereotype gay people into particular jobs such as artists, interior designers, hairdressers, but we are also your lawyers, teachers, doctors, nurses, police officers and fire-fighters. Some of us have faith and hope in Christ, some have no hope at all and toy with suicide everyday. It is very difficult to live in a world that doesn't accept you. It gets very lonely. All of us are human. All of us have been created by the One True God. The Lord wants us to have faith and accept ourselves the way that He accepts us (even though the world may reject us!). His love in unconditional.

Traci: It happens, gays can go straight, can't they?
Mary: That is debatable. There are people who think they may be homosexual. At some point they realize they are not gay; those people can "go straight" because they were never really gay. Maybe ex-gay ministries and other similar organizations can be helpful to them. Trying to change someone that is really gay is another story. Some gay people try to "become straight" because they cannot take the abuse, loneliness, and rejection from society. They feel it would be easier to be straight and fit in, just as it would be easier to be right-handed in a right-handed world. If you are left-handed, try to write, throw a ball, eat, or draw with your right hand. It can be done, but is it *natural* for you? Could you function normally and live a stable, productive life?

Can I go straight? No. Many straight people do not realize the damage they cause gay people by their constant rejection and disapproval, which are very unhealthy. Is it any wonder so many gay people are angry? But they continue to try to receive approval from their families, society, and the "church."

The only approval I value is God's. I already know it is impossible to please everyone. I have faith and confidence in Him....that is all that matters to me now. He loves me. I believe in Christ. *No one can take my faith away from me!* And the Bible says no one can separate me from the love of Christ! (Romans 8:35-39). The faith I have is a gift from God (Ephesians 2:8). I would never have been able to handle all the rejection and ridicule without Him.

Traci: I have many gay friends and I pray for them all the time. I try to talk to them about this, but I'm unsure how to approach them.
Mary: Good! Gay people, like everyone else, need people to pray for them. Love them in the Lord. Don't scare them. Teach them what you know about the unconditional love of God. Share your testimony with them. Leave the rest to God. Honestly, He can handle it from there. It is not our job to "save" people, only God can do that. Christians are supposed to be "ambassadors for Christ," called to share the good news of the gospel of reconciliation with *everyone* (2 Corinthians 5:20).

Traci: I pray that I don't make the same mistake as them.
Mary: You still don't "get it." Truly being gay is not a mistake, not by the person or by the Creator; we either are gay, or we're not. It is beyond our control, just as being left or right-handed is beyond our control.

Traci: I am not a gay basher by any means, but I find myself being confused about the whole issue.

Mary: I don't get the feeling that you are a gay basher, but the condemnation of gay people by some "Christians" trickles down to those who *are* gay bashers. Therein lies the danger for the gay person. Bible teachers and preachers have a multitude of people listening to them. Some listeners interpret these messages of condemnation as permission and blessing to judge and persecute gay people, in the name of Christ. Any intelligent person knows this is wrong and extremist.

When a minority is singled out as evil, perverted, and dangerous by organized religion, which incorrectly uses Scripture as its foundation, it is easy to see how this kind of elitist thinking can get out of hand. Hitler accused the Jewish people of similar traits and sold that thinking to the rest of his countrymen. The Germans, an educated, advanced and mostly Christian people, believed Hitler's lies, which led to the mass murder of millions of Jews, and, I might add, thousands of homosexuals. There were many churches and religious institutions that knew of, but did nothing to stop, the persecution and killing. Why do you think it is so hard to reach the Jewish people with the gospel? I have been told by a Holocaust survivor that the Nazi's wore crosses on their belt buckles! Many Jews to this day still think that Hitler was a Christian! Things can get easily out of control when messages of fear and blame are preached, because there are always people who are ready, willing, and able to take action against *the hated.*

Traci: I am just fearful for your eternal life. My Bible teacher says that homosexuality is a sin.

Mary: I appreciate your concern for me, but I trust in the living God. Besides, the Apostle John said that "...perfect love casts out fear"(1 John 4:18). I don't think it is good for you to be fearful, but to trust in God. You do not have to fear for me or anyone. God is the one that does the "saving," not you. You were not given that power or responsibility. We are all too small to handle the responsibility which is God's alone.

I do appreciate the fact that you are trying to understand this difficult issue. Many people that have been raised in church often mimic what they have heard, without much thought or personal study. The traditional, mainline, Christian denominations are becoming obsessed with this issue. Many homosexuals are frustrated and afraid of churches, because they feel that the predetermined minds of churchgoers are against them. It is beginning to feel like a crusade. It is preached in the pulpits, on the radio, on TV, and in books. So much valuable time to proclaim the gospel is being wasted on this obsession. Homosexuals are not the only ones sick of hearing it. There are many in the churches who are also tired of hearing it and who disagree with their ministers. Some are beginning to speak out.

A loving Christian that understands the will of God will prayerfully and thoughtfully think things through; only then can a person be seen for the individual they are, and not categorized into a stereotype. I am safe and loved by Jesus, much more so than by some who claim to be His followers.

Jesus was rejected and ostracized by His own people. He was crucified outside the gates of the city He loved, Jerusalem. He was rejected, ridiculed and despised. If the Lord was not accepted by his own people, then I am in great company when church doors are closed to me (see Hebrews 13:12-13).

If someone thinks that being with the same sex is wrong, then they shouldn't do it. Some things take time though to understand. God understands that also. "Work out your own salvation with fear and trembling" (Philippians 2:12). I really don't need anyone else working out my salvation for me. Do you?

Scripture says we are to love our neighbors (whoever they may be). Paul puts it all in proper perspective: "...for all have sinned and fall short of the glory of God" (Romans 3:23). Whether I am straight or gay, I will be a sinner for the rest of my life on earth. So will you. And so will all the preachers out there preaching that homosexuality is an abomination, a sin above all other sins. The Bible also says "All those who are arrogant are an abomination to the Lord..." (Proverbs 16:5, KJV). If it were not for the grace of God we would all be lost. Those of us who place our faith and trust in Christ have been saved by His grace alone (Ephesians 2:8); it is a gift from God.

Traci: Are you at peace with this Mary?
Mary: Traci, I have been "justified" by God because I have accepted and believe that Jesus is the Son of God. Romans 5:1 says that "...therefore, since we have been justified by faith, we have peace with God through our Lord Jesus Christ" (KJV). I have peace with God, Traci.

I appreciate your honest questions and interest in this difficult and complex issue. I hope my answers are thought provoking and clarify some of the misunderstandings. It would be a nicer world if there were more people like you.

Love in Christ,
Mary

Invitation

Would you like to be at peace with God?

Jesus died on the cross for all the sins
of the world, including yours.
He died, rose on the third day,
and ascended into heaven.
He is the way, the truth and the life.
He would like to direct your path and give you rest.
If you would like to invite the Lord Jesus Christ into
your heart, find peace, and experience
God's unconditional love,
please take a moment to say the simple prayer below.

*"Dear God, please have mercy on me, a sinner. I
invite your Son, Jesus, to be my Saviour, live in my
heart, and change my life. From this day forward,
I ask you to be my God and direct my steps.
Forgive me for my sins,
help me to follow Jesus (Yeshua*),
and guide me in the ways of truth.
In the name of Jesus, the Messiah, Amen."*

*Yeshua is the Hebrew word for Jesus.

Surprised By *peace*

ORDER FORM

PressOn Publications

P.O. Box 550363 • Ft. Lauderdale, FL 33355-0363

PressOn@BellSouth.Net • www.PressOnPublications.com

Please PRINT your name and complete mailing address below:

Name _____

Organization _____

Address _____

City _____ State _____ Zip _____

Phone (   )_____

E-Mail (optional) _____

Please make checks or money orders payable to: PressOn Publications.

Total copies _____ @ 12.99 each   =   _____

FL residents please add 6% sales tax   =   _____

Ship/Hand._____ @ $2.00 each   =   _____

TOTAL ENCLOSED   =   _____

Credit cards are accepted online using "PayPal"

Log on to: http://PressOnPublications.com

(Please allow 3-4 weeks for delivery)

Surprised By *peace*

ORDER FORM

PressOn Publications

P.O. Box 550363 • Ft. Lauderdale, FL 33355-0363

PressOn@BellSouth.Net • www.PressOnPublications.com

Please PRINT your name and complete mailing address below:

Name _____

Organization _____

Address _____

City_____ State_____ Zip _____

Phone (   )_____

E-Mail (optional) _____

Please make checks or money orders payable to: PressOn Publications.

Total copies _____ @ 12.99 each   =   _____

FL residents please add 6% sales tax   =   _____

Ship/Hand._____ @ $2.00 each   =   _____

TOTAL ENCLOSED   =   _____

Credit cards are accepted online using "PayPal"

Log on to: http://PressOnPublications.com

(Please allow 3-4 weeks for delivery)